# My First 1000 Words in SPANISH

Susan Martineau, Sam Hutchinson, Louise Millar and Catherine Bruzzone

Illustrations by Stu McLellan
Spanish adviser: Diego Blasco Vázquez

D1217883

## Sumario Contents
soo-*mah-reeyo*

b small publishing
www.bsmall.co.uk

disc

**la pluma**
la *plooma*
pen

**el futbolín**
el footbol-*een*
table football

**el niño/
la niña**
el *neen*-yo/la *neen*-ya
child

**el rincón
de lectura**
el reen-*kon* deh lek-*toora*
reading corner

**la pizarra**
la peeth-*ah*-rah
whiteboard

**los gemelos/
las gemelas**
loss he*meh*-loss/lass he*meh*-lass
twins

**el libro de texto**
el *leebro* deh *texto*
textbook

**el profesor/
la profesora**
el pro*fessor*/la pro*fessora*
teacher

**la puerta**
la *pwairta*
door

# En la escuela
en la esk*weh*-la
## At school

**el reloj**
el re*lokh*
clock

**la estantería**
la ess-tant-air-ee-a
bookshelf

**la tablet**
la *tah*-blet
tablet

**la merienda**
la meh-ree-*enda*
snack

**las tijeras**
las tee-*hair*-ass
scissors

**la cartera**
la kar*tair*-a
satchel

**el ordenador**
el ordenad-*dor*
computer

**la silla**
la *see-ya*
chair

**la clase**
la *klass*-eh
classroom

**la regla**
la *reh*-gla
ruler

**los lápices de colores**
loss *lap-eethess deh kol-or-ess*
coloured pencils

**el alfabeto**
el *alfabeh*-to
alphabet

**el pegamento**
el *peg-amento*
glue

**el juego**
el *hway*-go
game

**el cuadro**
el *kwah*-dro
painting

**el pincel**
el *peen-thel*
paintbrush

**el papel**
el *pap-el*
paper

**el alumno/
la alumna**
el *aloom*-no/la *aloom*-na
pupil

**la mochila**
la *mochee*-la
rucksack

**las pinturas**
las *peen-too-rass*
paints

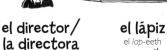
**el pupitre**
el *poopee-treh*
desk

**el póster**
el *postair*
poster

**el director/
la directora**
el *deer-ek-tor*/la *deer-ek-tora*
head teacher

**la goma de borrar**
la *gom-a deh borrar*
rubber

**el lápiz**
el *lap*-eeth
pencil

3

# El parque

el *parkeh*

## The park

**la cometa**
la komeh-ta
kite

**el carrito**
el kar-eeto
pushchair

**la pluma**
la ploo-ma
feather

**el árbol**
el *ar*-bol
tree

**el puente**
el *pwen*-teh
bridge

**el renacuajo**
el rayna-*kwa*-ho
tadpole

**el buho**
el *boo*-ho
owl

**el minigolf**
el mee-nee-*golf*
mini-golf

**el columpio**
el koloom-peeo
swing

**el palo**
el *pah*-lo
stick

**el tobogán**
el tobo-*gan*
slide

**el pony**
el *poh*-nay
pony

**el balancín**
el balan-*theen*
see-saw

**el cajón de arena**
el ka-*hon* deh ah-*rayna*
sandpit

**el bote a remos**
el *boteh* ah *raymoss*
rowing boat

**el ping pong**
el peeng-*pong*
table tennis

**los patines**
loss pat-ee-ness
rollerblades

4

**el banco**
el *ban-ko*
bench

**el matorral**
el *mat-oh-ral*
bush

**palos para trepar**
*paloss pah-*ra treh-*par*
climbing frame

**la valla**
la *va-*yah
fence

**la rana**
la *rah-*na
frog

**el amigo/**
**la amiga**
el amee-go/
la amee-ga
friend

**los amigos/**
**las amigas**
loss amee-goss/
lass a-mee-gass
friends

**el niño**
el *neen-*yo
boy

**la niña**
la *neen-*ya
girl

**el ganso**
el *gan-*so
goose

**el corredor/**
**la corredora**
el koreh-*dor*/la koreh-*dora*
jogger

**el jardinero**
el hardee-*nairo*
park-keeper

**el arroyo**
el ah-*roy-*o
stream

**el parque infantil**
el *par-*keh eenfan-*teel*
playground

**el palomo**
el pah-*lo-*moh
pigeon

**la cuerda de saltar**
la *kwair-*da deh sal-*tar*
skipping rope

**el tronco**
el *tron-*koh
log

**la glorieta**
la gloree-etta
pavilion

**la piscina**
**de niños**
la pee-*thee-*na deh *neen-*yoss
paddling pool

**el remo**
el *ray-*mo
oar

5

**el loro**
el loro
parrot

**el tigre**
el tee-greh
tiger

# En el zoo
en el thoh
# At the zoo

**la cebra**
la theb-ra
zebra

**el lagarto**
el lagar-to
lizard

**el mono**
el mon-o
monkey

**el refugio**
el reh-foo-heeo
shelter

**la cuerda**
la kwair-dah
rope

**el hipopótamo**
el eepo-pot-amo
hippopotamus

**el oso polar**
el osso polar
polar bear

**la morsa**
la mor-sah
walrus

**el reno**
el ray-no
reindeer

**el pingüino**
el peen-gweeno
penguin

**la serpiente**
la sairp-yen-teh
snake

**el panda**
el panda
panda

**la nutria**
la noo-tree-a
otter

**el rinoceronte**
el reeno-thairon-teh
rhinoceros

**el suricato**
el sooree-kato
meerkat

6

**el aviario**
el avee-*ah*-ree-o
aviary

**el león**
el lay-*on*
lion

**el koala**
el ko-*wah*-la
koala

**el canguro**
el kan-goo-ro
kangaroo

**la jirafa**
la hee-*rah*-fa
giraffe

**los animales**
loss anee-*mah*-less
animals

**el cactus**
el *kak*-toos
cactus

**el mapache**
el ma*pa*-cheh
racoon

**el elefante**
el eleh-*fan*-teh
elephant

**el camaleón**
el kama-leh-*on*
chameleon

**la madriguera**
la mad-ree-*gwair*-a
burrow

**el gorila**
el go-ree-la
gorilla

**el oso pardo**
el osso *par*-do
grizzly bear

**el cocodrilo**
el kokko-*dree*-lo
crocodile

**el murciélago**
el moorthee-*eh*-lago
bat

**el castor**
el kass-*tor*
beaver

**el lobo**
el *lo*-bo
wolf

**la jungla**
la *hoon*-gla
jungle

**la jaula**
la *how*-la
cage

**7**

**el tractor**
el trak-*tor*
tractor

**el remolque**
el remol-keh
trailer

# La granja
la *gran*-ha

## The farm

**el prado**
el *prah*-do
field

**las botas
de agua**
lass *botass* deh *awa*
wellington boots

**la escoba**
la es-*ko*-ba
broom

**el bebedero**
el bebe-*dair*-o
trough

**el perro pastor**
el *peh*-ro pass-*tor*
sheepdog

**el pastor**
el pass-*tor*
shepherd

**el espantapájaros**
el esspanta-*pahaross*
scarecrow

**el heno**
el *eh*-no
hay

**el patio**
el *patee*-o
yard

**la rata**
la *rah*-ta
rat

**el conejo**
el kon-*eh*-ho
rabbit

**el saco**
el *sah*-ko
sack

**el quad**
el kwad
quadbike

**el cerdito**
el thair-*deet*-o
piglet

**el cerdo**
el *thaird*-o
pig

**el panal**
el *panal*
beehive

**el pato**
el *pat*-o
duck

**el patito**
el *pateet*-o
duckling

**el fango**
el *fan*-go
mud

**el ternero**
el tair-*nairo*
calf

**la vaca**
la *bak*-a
cow

**la gallina**
la ga-*yeen*-a
chicken

**el pollito**
el *poyeet*-o
chick

**el granero**
el gran-*airo*
barn

**el cuervo**
el *kwair*-bo
crow

**el tejón**
el teh-*hon*
badger

**la granja**
la *gran*-ha
farmhouse

**el trigo**
el *tree*-go
wheat

**el huerto**
el *wairt*-oh
orchard

**la cabra**
la *kab*-ra
goat

**el cabrito**
el ka-*bree*-to
kid

**el cordero**
el kor*dair*-o
lamb

**la oveja**
la o-*veh*-ha
sheep

**el potro**
el *pot*-ro
foal

**el caballo**
el ka-*bah*-yo
horse

**la cosechadora**
la koseh-*chadora*
combine harvester

9

**la vajilla sucia**
la baheeya suthea
washing up

**el cereal**
el thair-eh-*al*
cereal

# La cocina
la ko*thee*-na
## The kitchen

**la tetera**
la teh-*taira*
teapot

**la tacita**
la ta-*thee*-ta
beaker

**la lavadora**
la laba*dor*-ra
washing machine

**el plato**
el *plat*-o
plate

**el platillo**
el plat-ee-yo
saucer

**la tostada**
la tost-*ada*
toast

**los pañuelos**
loss pan-*way*-lass
tissues

**el cuchillo**
el koochee-yo
knife

**el paño de cocina**
el *pan*-yo deh ko*thee*-na
tea towel

**la cuchara**
la koo*char*-a
spoon

**la mesa**
la *messa*
table

**la cacerola**
la katheh-*ro*-la
saucepan

**el té**
el teh
tea

**el fregadero**
el frega-*dair*-o
sink

**el taburete**
el taboo-*reh*-teh
stool

**el agua**
el awa
water

**el café**
el ka-*feh*
coffee

**el babero**
el ba*bair*-o
bib

**la taza**
la *tath*-a
cup

**la huevera**
la way-*bair*-a
egg cup

**la ventana**
la b*entana*
window

**el tazón**
el tath-*on*
bowl

**el desayuno**
el dessa-*yoo*-no
breakfast

**el delantal**
el deh-lan-*tal*
apron

**la cocina**
la ko-*thee*-na
cooker

**el tenedor**
el teneh-*dor*
fork

**el frigorífico**
el freegoree-feeko
fridge

**el vaso**
el *bah*-so
glass

**la trona**
la *tro*-na
highchair

**la pasta**
la *pas*-ta
pasta

**el zumo de naranja**
el *thoo*-mo deh nar-*an*-ha
orange juice

**la leche**
la *leh*-cheh
milk

**la carta**
la *kar*-ta
letter

**la mermelada**
la mairmeh-*lah*-da
jam

**el wok**
el wok
wok

# El huerto

el *hwair*-to

## The garden

**la casita del árbol**
la *kasseeta* del *ar*-bol
treehouse

**la carretilla**
la *karreh-tee*-ya
wheelbarrow

**la flor**
la flor
flower

**la hoja**
la *o*-ha
leaf

**la lombriz**
*lombreeth*
worm

**la regadera**
la *regadair*-a
watering-can

**la cisterna pluvial**
la *theess-taima* ploovee-*al*
water butt

**el caracol**
el *karakol*
snail

**la madera**
la *madair*-a
wood

**el hacha**
el *ah*-cha
axe

**el rastrillo**
el *rass-tree*-yo
rake

**la araña**
la *aran*-ya
spider

**el muro**
el *moo*-ro
wall

**el cobertizo**
el *kobair-teetho*
shed

**el serrucho**
el *sair-oocho*
saw

**la paleta**
la *paleh*-ta
trowel

**el estanque**
el *ess-tankeh*
pond

**el camino**
el *kam-een-o*
path

12

**el manzano**
el man*than*-o
apple tree

**el seto**
el *seh*-to
hedge

**el césped**
el *thess*-ped
lawn

**la puerta de la verja**
la p*wair*ta deh la *bair*-ha
gate

**la cesta**
la *thess*ta
basket

**la rama**
la *rama*
branch

**el garaje**
el gar-*rah*-heh
garage

**el compost**
el kom*post*
compost heap

**la hierba**
la *yair*-ba
grass

**el invernadero**
el een-bair-na*dair*-o
greenhouse

**el martillo**
el mar-*tee*-yo
hammer

**el comedero de pájaros**
el komed-*airo* deh *paha*ross
bird feeder

**la manguera**
la man-*gair*-a
hose

**el cortacésped**
el korta-*thess*-ped
lawnmower

**el clavo**
el *klav*-o
nail

**la caja de herramientas**
la *caha* deh errah-mee-entas
toolbox

**la maceta**
la *matheh*-ta
plant pot

**el huerto**
el *hwairto*
vegetable garden

**el gatito**
el *gateet*-o
kitten

**la escalera**
la eska-*lair*-a
ladder

# El baño y el dormitorio

el *ban*-yo ee el dormee*tor*-eeo

## Bathroom and bedroom

### la ducha
la *doocha*
shower

### la toalla
la toh-*wah*-ya
towel

### el lavabo
el la-*bah*-bo
washbasin

### la pasta de dientes
la *pas*-tah deh dee-*yen*-tess
toothpaste

### el cepillo de dientes
el thep-ee-yo deh dee-*yen*-tess
toothbrush

### el retrete
el reh-*treh*-teh
toilet

### el papel higiénico
el pa*pel* eeyeneeko
toilet paper

### el despertado
el despairta-*dor*
alarm clock

### la bañera
la banyair-a
bath

### la esponja
la ess*pon*-ha
sponge

### el jabón
el ha*bon*
soap

### el champú
el sham-*poo*
shampoo

### la sábana
la *sabana*
sheet

### la almohada
al almo*hah*-da
pillow

### el móvil
el *mo*-veel
mobile phone

14

**el osito de peluche**
el osseeto deh peloocheh
teddy bear

**la cama**
la kah-ma
bed

**la mesita de noche**
la meh-seeta deh nocheh
bedside table

**la cómoda**
la kom-oda
chest of drawers

**la manta**
la manta
blanket

**el armario**
el armar-eeyo
wardrobe

**la cuna**
la koona
cot

**las cortinas**
las kor-teen-ass
curtains

**la lámpara**
la lam-para
desk lamp

**la colcha**
la kolcha
duvet

**el cepillo del pelo**
el thep-ee-yo del peh-lo
hairbrush

**el hámster**
el amstair
hamster

**el espejo**
el espeh-ho
mirror

**la alfombrilla**
la alfom-breeya
mat

**el joyero**
el hoyairo
jewellery box

**los auriculares**
loss ah-oo-ree-koo lar-ess
headphones

**la casa**
la kah-sa
house

**el peine**
el payee-neh
comb

**el baúl**
el bah-ool
trunk

**el apartamento**
el apar-tamento
apartment

**el teléfono**
el teh-*leh*-fono
telephone

**el aspirador**
el aspeera-*dor*
vacuum cleaner

**la televisión**
la tele-veezee-*on*
television

**la madriguera del ratón**
el mehdree-*gwair*-ah del rat*on*
mouse hole

**las manchas**
las *manchass*
stains

**los altavoces**
loss alta-*vothess*
speakers

**el sofá**
el sof-*a*
sofa

# En casa
en *kas*-sa
# At home

**los muebles**
los *mweb*-less
furniture

**el salón**
el sal-*on*
sitting room

**la radio**
la *rad*-eeo
radio

**la alfombra**
la al-*fom*-bra
rug

**el perro**
el *pe*-roh
dog

**la jarra de agua**
la *harra* deh *ag*-wa
jug of water

**el reposapiés**
el repohsah-pee-ess
footstool

**el cuadro**
el *kwad*-dro
picture

**la botella**
la bo*tay*-a
bottle

**la servilleta**
la sairvee-*et*-a
napkin

**el techo**
el *teh*-cho
ceiling

**el posavasos**
el possa-*basoss*
coaster

**la alacena**
el ala*thay*-na
cupboard

**el cojín**
el ko*heen*
cushion

**el comedor**
el komed-*or*
dining room

**el cachorro**
el ka*chor*-o
puppy

**el aparador**
el apara-*dor*
dresser

**el DVD**
el deh-veh-*deh*
DVD

**la planta**
la *plan*-ta
plant

**el sillón**
el see-*yon*
armchair

**el florero**
el flor-*airo*
vase

**el suelo**
el *sweh*-lo
floor

**la llave**
la *yah*-veh
key

**el mando a distancia**
el man-do a diss-*tansseah*
remote control

**el gato**
el *gat*-o
cat

**el ratón**
el rat-*on*
mouse

**la comida**
la komee-da
meal

**el portátil**
el por*tat*-eel
laptop

**la pantalla**
la pan*tah*-ya
lampshade

**la lámpara**
la *lam*-para
lamp

17

# La playa y el fondo del mar

la *plah*-ya ee el *fondo* del mar

## Beach and under the sea

**el faro**
el *fah*-ro
lighthouse

**la gaviota**
la gab-*yota*
seagull

**la ballena**
la bah-*yena*
whale

**la ola**
la *oh*-la
wave

**el traje de baño**
el *tra*-heh deh *banyo*
swimming costume

**el chaleco salvavidas**
el *chaleko* salva-vee-dass
lifejacket

**las gafas de sol**
las *gah*-fass deh sol
sunglasses

**la loción solar**
la *lothee-on* solar
suncream

**el castillo de arena**
el kastee-yo deh ah-*rayna*
sandcastle

**la pala**
la *pah*-la
spade

**la concha**
la *koncha*
shell

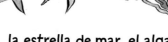

**el tiburón**
el teeboo-*ron*
shark

**la estrella de mar**
la estreh-ya deh mar
starfish

**el alga marina**
el *alga* mareena
seaweed

**la tabla de surf**
la *tabla* deh soorf
surfboard

**el/la surfista**
el/la soor-*feesta*
surfer

18

**el cangrejo**
el kangreh-ho
crab

**el cubo**
el koo-bo
bucket

**la boya**
la boy-a
buoy

**el barco de pesca**
el barko deh peska
fishing boat

**las patatas fritas**
las patat-ass freetass
chips

**la tumbona**
la toombona
deckchair

**la sombrilla**
la sombree-ya
beach umbrella

**el acantilado**
el akanteelad-o
cliff

**el buceador/
la buceadora**
el bookeh-ador
la bookeh-adora
diver

**el coral**
el koral
coral

**el delfín**
el del-feen
dolphin

**el pez**
el peth
fish

**el algodón
de azúcar**
el algo-don deh
athoo-kar
candyfloss

**la medusa**
la medoo-sa
jellyfish

**la arena**
la ah-rayna
sand

**el pulpo**
el pool-po
octopus

**el naufragio**
el now-frah-hee-o
wreck

**la langosta**
la langoo-sta
lobster

**la pelota
de playa**
la peh-lot-a
beach ball

**el velero**
el bel-lairo
yacht

**el salvavidas**
el salva-vee-dass
rubber ring

**el bote**
el boteh
dinghy

19

# En el campo
en el *kampo*
## In the countryside

**el campamento**
el kampa-*mento*
campsite

**el bastón**
el *baston*
walking stick

**las botas**
lass *botass*
walking boots

**el sendero**
el sen*dairo*
track

**la viña**
la *been*-ya
vineyard

**la tienda de campaña**
la tee-enda deh kam*pan*-ya
tent

**el río**
el *ree*-o
river

**la cascada**
la kass*kah*-da
waterfall

**la ardilla**
la ar*dee*-ya
squirrel

**el cartel**
el *car*-tell
signpost

**el picnic**
el *peek*-neek
picnic

**el bocadillo**
el boka*dee*-yo
sandwich

**el escarabajo**
el eskah-rah-*bah*-ho
beetle

**los prismáticos**
loss prees-*mateekoss*
binoculars

**la roca**
la *roka*
rock

**el remo**
el *reh*-mo
paddle

**la mountain bike**
la *moonten* bike
mountain bike

**el pájaro**
el *pa*-haro
bird

**el oso pardo**
el osso *pardo*
brown bear

**la mariposa**
la maree-*posa*
butterfly

**las piedras**
lass pee-*edrass*
stones

**la grulla**
la *groo*-ya
crane

**la piragua**
la peer-*agwa*
canoe

**la oruga**
la *oroo*-ga
caterpillar

**el cisne**
el *theesneh*
swan

**el cisne pequeñito**
el *theesneh* peken-*yeet*-o
cygnet

**el ciervo**
el thee-*air*-bo
deer

**el fuego**
el foo-*eh*-go
fire

**pescar**
pess-*kar*
fishing

**la mosca**
la *moss*-ka
fly

**el bosque**
el *boss*-keh
forest

**el zorro**
el *thor*-ro
fox

**la colina**
la *koleena*
hill

**la montaña**
la mon-*tan*-ya
mountain

**el mosquito**
el moss-*keet*-o
mosquito

**el mapa**
el *mapa*
map

**el lago**
el *lah*-go
lake

**el dia festivo**
el *dee*-a festeevo
holiday

21

# La tienda de libros y juguetes

la tee-*en*da deh *leebross* ee hoo*get*-ess

## Bookshop and toyshop

**los bloques**
loss *blok*-ess
blocks

**el xilófono**
el see-*lo*-fono
xylophone

**la trompeta**
la trom*peh*-ta
trumpet

**el triciclo**
el tree-*thee*-klo
tricycle

**los juguetes**
loss hoo*get*-ess
toys

**la caja
registradora**
la *kah*-ha
reh-heestra*dor*-a
till

**el disfraz
de superhéroe**
el deess*frath*
deh sooper-*airo*-eh
superhero
costume

**los dados**
loss *dahd*-oss
dice

**el robot**
el rob-*ot*
robot

**el libro de cuentos**
el *leebro* deh koo-en-toss
storybook

**la maqueta
de avión**
la *makeh*-ta deh abee-*on*
model aeroplane

**el rompecabezas**
el rompeh-*kabeth*-ass
jigsaw

**la estantería**
la esstantairee-a
shelf

**el caballito
balancín**
el kabayeet-o balan-*theen*
rocking horse

**el libro**
el *leebro*
book

**los peluches**
loss *peloochess*
cuddly toys

**los platillos**
loss *platee-yoss*
cymbals

**el castillo**
el *kastee-yo*
castle

**el tambor**
el *tambor*
drum

**el diccionario**
el *deex-theeonar-eeo*
dictionary

**la casa de muñecas**
la *kas-sa deh moon-yekass*
doll's house

**la muñeca**
la *moon-yeh-ka*
doll

**el dominó**
el domee-*no*
dominoes

**los zancos**
loss *thankoss*
stilts

**el globo terráqueo**
el *globo* tairah-keh-o
globe

**la guitarra**
la gee*tar*-ra
guitar

**los títeres**
loss *teet-eh-ress*
puppets

**el monedero**
el moned-*air*-o
purse

**la flauta**
la *fla*-oo-ta
recorder

**el trenecito de juguete**
el treneh-*theet*-o deh hooget-eh
toy train

**el juego de magia**
el hoo-eh-go deh *maheea*
magic set

**el dinero**
el *deenairo*
money

**la tienda**
la tee-*enda*
shop

23

# Transporte
transporteh
## Transport

**los vehículos**
loss beh-hee-kooloss
vehicles

**la furgoneta**
la foorgoneh-ta
van

**el túnel**
el toonel
tunnel

**el barco**
el barko
boat

**el billete**
el bee-yet-eh
ticket

**el ferry**
el fairee
ferry

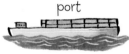

**el puerto**
el pwairto
port

**el portacontenedores**
el poor-tah konteneh-dores
container ship

 **la maleta**
la maleh-ta
suitcase

  **la señal**
la senyal
signal

**el aeropuerto**
el ah-air-o-pwairto
airport

**el barco**
el barko
ship

**el asiento**
el assee-ento
seat

**el tren**
el tren
train

**los raíles**
loss rah-ee-less
rails

**la estación de tren**
la esstathee-on deh tren
rail station

**el paso a nivel**
el pah-so ah neebel
level crossing

**el avión**
el abee-*on*
aeroplane

**la excavadora**
la eskaba-*dor*-a
digger

**el dúmper**
el doom-*pair*
dumper truck

**el ladrillo**
el ladree-yo
brick

**el bulldozer**
el bool-*doth*-air
bulldozer

**el helicóptero**
el elee-*koptairo*
helicopter

**el camión hormigonera**
lel kam-*yon*
ormee-gon-*aira*
cement mixer

**el andamio**
el an*dah*-mee-o
scaffolding

**la escalera mecánica**
la eska*laira* mek*aneeka*
escalator

**el autobús**
el ah-oto-*boos*
bus

**el coche de bomberos**
el kocheh deh bom*bair*-oss
fire engine

**el ascensor**
el ass-*thensor*
lift

**el andén**
el an*den*
platform

**la motocicleta**
la moto-thee-*klet*-a
motorbike

**el coche de policía**
el *kocheh* deh polee-*thee*-ya
police car

**el equipaje**
el ekee-*pah*-heh
luggage

**el camión**
el kamy-*on*
lorry

**la obra**
la *ob*-ra
building site

25

# En la ciudad
en la theeoo-*dad*

## In town

**la rotonda**
la roton-da
roundabout

**el cine**
el *theeneh*
cinema

**el cartero**
el kar*tair*-o
postman

**la bolsa del cartero**
la bolssa del kar*tair*-o
postbag

**el buzón**
el boo*thon*
postbox

**la oficina de correos**
la ofee-*thee*-na deh korr-*eh*-oss
post office

**el semáforo**
el se*mah*-foro
traffic lights

**la panadería**
la panadairee-a
bakery

**el paso de peatones**
el *pah*-so deh pay-*atoness*
pedestrian crossing

**la tienda de mascotas**
le tee-*enda* deh masskotass
petshop

**la carretera**
la *kah-retair*-ah
road

**el váter público**
el *bah*-tair poobleeko
toilets

**el paraguas**
el par-*ag*-was
umbrella

**el tenderete**
el tendaireh-teh
stall

**el restaurante**
el resta-o-*ranteh*
restaurant

**el coche**
el *kocheh*
car

**la fábrica**
la *fab*-reeka
factory

**la bicicleta**
la bee-thee-*klet*-a
bicycle

**la papelera**
la pape*laira*
bin

**la acera**
la ah-*thair*-a
pavement

**la bandera**
la band*aira*
flag

**la carnicería**
la karneeth-airee-a
butcher's

**el café**
el *kafeh*
café

**la farmacia**
la farm*athee*-a
chemist

**el banco**
el *banko*
bank

**el hotel**
el *otel*
hotel

**la biblioteca**
la beebleeo-*teka*
library

**la gasolinera**
la gassoleen*air*-a
petrol station

**la parada del bus**
la pa*rada* del *booss*
bus stop

**la oficina**
la ofee-*thee*-na
office

**el museo**
el moo-*seh*-o
museum

**la señal de tráfico**
la *senyal* deh *trafeeko*
road sign

**el mercado**
el mair-*kad*-o
market

27

**la bruja**
la *broo-ha*
witch

**la tiara**
la *tee-ah-ra*
tiara

# La fiesta
la *fee-esthah*
## Party

**las salchichas**
lass *salchee-chass*
sausages

**el globo**
el *globo*
balloon

**el violín**
el *beeyo-leen*
violin

**la serpentina**
la *sairpentee-na*
streamer

**la reina**
la *ray-eena*
queen

**la princesa**
la *preen-thessa*
princess

**el príncipe**
el *preen-thee-peh*
prince

**la sirena**
la *seeray-na*
mermaid

**el pirata**
el *peerah-ta*
pirate

**el sombrero de fiesta**
el *sombrairo deh fee-ess-ta*
party hat

**el vestido de fiesta**
el *vesteedo deh fee-ess-ta*
party dress

**el matasuegras**
el *matasoo-egrass*
party blower

**el gigante**
el *heeganteh*
giant

**la música**
la *mooseeka*
music

28

**las magdalenas**
las magda-*leh*-nass
cupcakes

**el collar de cuentas**
el koh-*yar* deh *kwentas*
beads

**el helado**
el e*lad*-o
ice-cream

**la pizza**
la *peet*-za
pizza

**el regalo**
el re*gal*-o
present

**el chocolate**
el chokko-*lah*-teh
chocolate

**el hada**
el *ah*-da
fairy

**el refresco**
el re*fressko*
cola

**la corona**
la *korona*
crown

**la vela**
la *bay*-la
candle

**el caballero**
el kaba-*yair*-o
knight

**la capa**
la *kah*-pa
cloak

**las zapatillas de ballet**
la thapatee-yass deh bah-yet
ballet shoes

**el genio**
el *haynee*-o
genie

**el rey**
el ray
king

**el zumo de fruta**
el *thoomo* deh *froota*
fruit juice

**la varita mágica**
la *baree*-ta *ma*-heeka
magic wand

**la limonada**
la *leemonah*-da
lemonade

**la piruleta**
la *peeroo*-*lay*-ta
lollipop

**la lámpara mágica**
la *lampara ma*-heeka
magic lamp

**el dragón**
el *drag-on*
dragon

29

# El supermercado

## The supermarket

**las verduras**
lass bair-doo-rass
vegetables

**la manzana**
la man-thah-na
apple

**el yogur**
el yog-oor
yogurt

**el carrito**
el kareeto
trolley

**el tomate**
el tom-ah-teh
tomato

**la fresa**
la fray-sa
strawberry

**la bolsa de
la compra**
la bolsa deh lah kompra
shopping bag

**la ensalada**
la ensa-lah-da
salad

**el arroz**
el ah-roth
rice

**la patata**
la pat-ah-ta
potato

**la piña**
la peen-ya
pineapple

**la pera**
la pair-a
pear

**el melocotón**
el melo-koton
peach

**la naranja**
la nah-ran-ha
orange

**la cebolla**
la theh-boy-a
onion

**el mango**
el mango
mango

**el limón**
el leemon
lemon

**la lechuga**
la leh-choo-ga
lettuce

**la berenjena**
la bairen-*hay*-na
aubergine

**el plátano**
el *plah*-tan-o
banana

**las galletas**
las gah-*yeh*-tass
biscuits

**el pan**
el pan
bread

**la mantequilla**
la manteh-kee-ya
butter

**la col**
la kol
cabbage

**el pastel**
el pass-*tel*
cake

**la zanahoria**
la thanah-or-ee-a
carrot

**el apio**
el *ah*-pee-o
celery

**el queso**
el *keh*-soh
cheese

**la cereza**
la theh-*reh*-tha
cherry

**el pollo**
el *po*-yo
chicken

**el maíz**
el mah-*eeth*
corn

**el calabacín**
el kalaba-*theen*
courgette

**el pepino**
el pe*peeno*
cucumber

**el kiwi**
el *kee*-wee
kiwi

**el jamón**
el ha*mon*
ham

**las uvas**
lass *oobass*
grapes

**la fruta**
la *froo*-ta
fruit

**la comida**
la ko-*mee*-da
food

**el pescado**
el pes*kad*-o
fish

**los huevos**
los *way*-boss
eggs

31

# En el centro deportivo
en el *then*tro deh-*por*teevoh
## At the sports centre

**los deportes**
loss dep-*or*tess
sport

**la carrera**
la ka*rair*-a
race

**el yoga**
el *yoga*
yoga

**el silbato**
el seel*bat*-o
whistle

**la silla de ruedas**
la *seeya* deh roo-eh-dass
wheelchair

**la cancha de tenis**
la *kancha* deh *ten*-eess
tennis court

**el tenis**
el *ten*-eess
tennis

**el equipo**
el ek-*eepo*
team

**el taco de salida**
el *tak*-o deh sa*leeda*
starting block

**el equipo
de deporte**
el ek-*eepo* deh deh-*porteh*
sports kit

**la bolsa
de deporte**
la *bolssa* deh deh-*porteh*
sports bag

**la piscina**
la *peess-theena*
swimming-pool

**nadar**
nah-*dar*
swimming

**los esquís**
los ess-*keess*
skis

**esquiar**
ess-kee-*ar*
skiing

**el volante**
el bo*lanteh*
shuttlecock

## los aerobics
*loss ah-airo-beeks*
aerobics

## el badminton
*el bad-meenton*
badminton

## el atletismo
*el atlet-eesmo*
athletics

## el baloncesto
*el balon-thess-sto*
basketball

## el vestuario
*el bestooah-ree-o*
changing-room

## el partido de fútbol
*el parteedo deh footbol*
football match

## el trampolín
*el trampoleen*
diving board

## el balón de fútbol
*el balon deh footbol*
football

## la raqueta
*la raketa*
racket

## el entrenador/
## la entrenadora
*el entrenador/la entrenadora*
coach

## la pelota
*la peh-lot-a*
ball

## las gafas
## de natación
*lass gafass deh natathee-on*
goggles

## la gimnasia
*la him-nass-eea*
gymnastics

## el marcador
*el markad-or*
scoreboard

## la sauna
*la sah-oona*
sauna

## el/la árbitro
*el/la ar-beetro*
referee

## el portero
*el portair-o*
goalkeeper

## el salto de altura
*el salto deh altoora*
high jump

## el salto de longitud
*el salto deh lon-gee-tood*
long jump

# Palabras de hacer

palabrass deh athair

## Doing words

**estar de pie**
esstar deh pee-eh
standing

**ver la tele**
vair la teh-leh
watching TV

**hablar**
ablar
talking

**cocinar**
kothee-nar
cooking

**estar sentado**
esstar sentad-o
sitting

**lavar los dientes**
lavar loss dee-entess
cleaning your teeth

**llevar**
yev-ar
carrying

**andar**
andar
walking

**empujar**
empoo-har
pushing

**tirar**
teer-ar
pulling

**señalar**
sen-yal-ar
pointing

**jugar**
hoo-gar
playing

**pintar**
peen-tar
painting

**saltar**
sal-tar
jumping

34

**leer**
leh-*air*
reading

**cantar**
kantar
singing

**dibujar**
deeboo-*har*
drawing

**escribir**
esskree-*beer*
writing

**gatear**
gah-*tay*-ah
crawling

**montar en bicicleta**
montar en beetheekleta
cycling

**bailar**
bah-ee-*lar*
dancing

**hacer la rueda**
athair la roo-ed-a
doing a cartwheel

**hacer el pino**
athair el peeno
doing a handstand

**dar volteretas**
dar voltair-ret-ass
doing somersaults

**escalar**
eskal-*ar*
climbing

**beber**
beh-*bair*
drinking

**comer**
komair
eating

**besar**
besar
kissing

**abrazar**
abrah-*thar*
hugging

**lavarse**
la*bar*-seh
having a wash

**correr**
kor-*air*
running

**acostarse**
akostar-seh
going to sleep

**levantarse**
leban*tar*-seh
getting up

35

# Tu cuerpo

too koo-*airpo*

## Your body

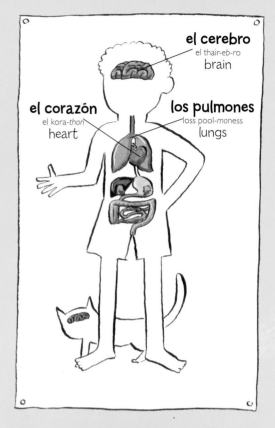

**el cerebro**
el thair-*eb*-ro
brain

**el corazón**
el kora-*thon*
heart

**los pulmones**
loss pool-*moness*
lungs

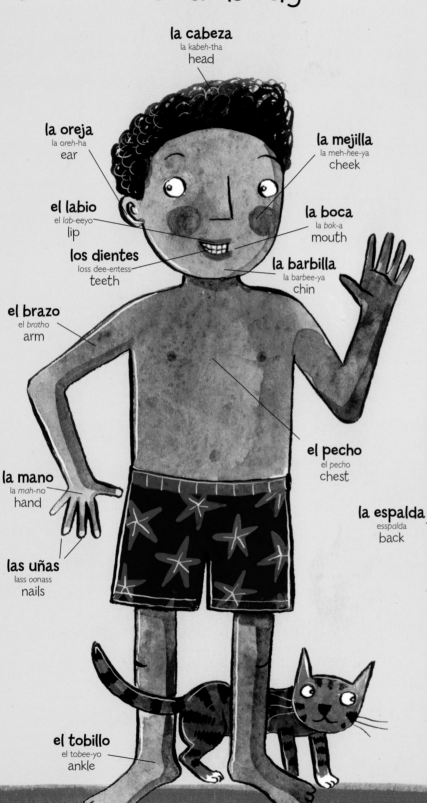

**la cabeza**
la kabeh-tha
head

**la oreja**
la oreh-ha
ear

**la mejilla**
la meh-hee-ya
cheek

**el labio**
el *lab*-eeyo
lip

**la boca**
la *bok*-a
mouth

**los dientes**
loss dee-*entess*
teeth

**la barbilla**
la barbee-ya
chin

**el brazo**
el *bratho*
arm

**la mano**
la *mah*-no
hand

**las uñas**
lass oonass
nails

**el pecho**
el *pecho*
chest

**el tobillo**
el tobee-yo
ankle

**la espalda**
ess*palda*
back

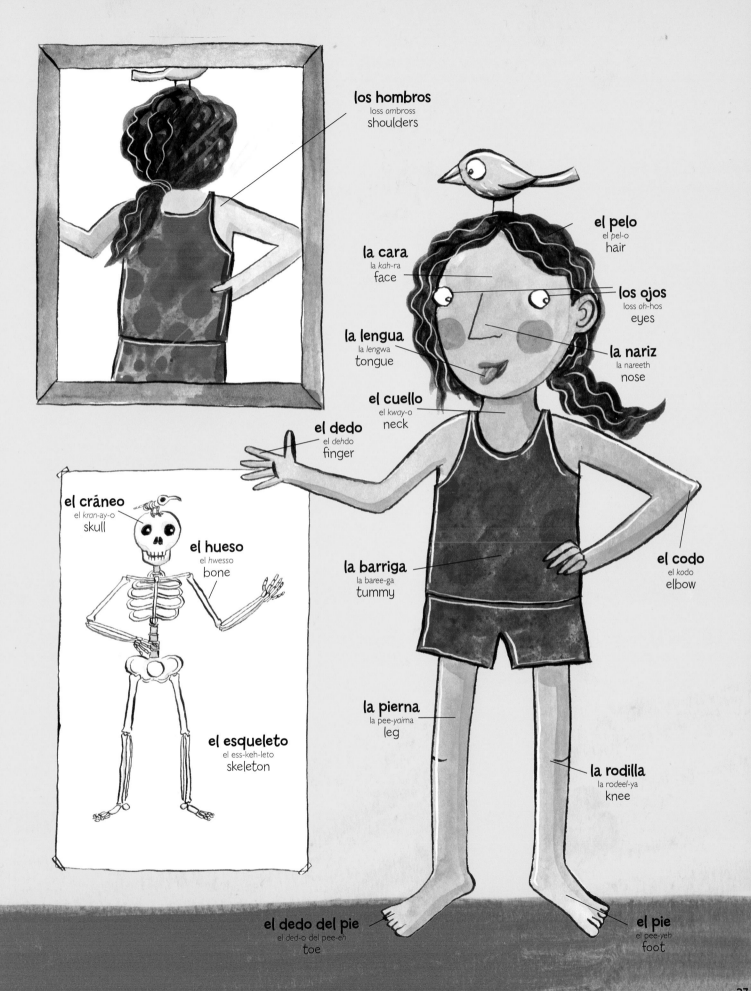

**los hombros**
loss ombross
shoulders

**el pelo**
el *pel*-o
hair

**la cara**
la *kah*-ra
face

**los ojos**
loss *oh*-hos
eyes

**la lengua**
la *lengwa*
tongue

**la nariz**
la *nareeth*
nose

**el cuello**
el *kway*-o
neck

**el dedo**
el *dehdo*
finger

**el cráneo**
el *kran-ay-o*
skull

**el hueso**
el *hwesso*
bone

**la barriga**
la *baree-ga*
tummy

**el codo**
el *kodo*
elbow

**el esqueleto**
el *ess-keh-leto*
skeleton

**la pierna**
la *pee-yaima*
leg

**la rodilla**
la *rodeel-ya*
knee

**el dedo del pie**
el *ded-o* del *pee-eh*
toe

**el pie**
el *pee-yeh*
foot

# Colores y formas

## Colours and shapes

**el caballete**
el kaba-yeh-teh
easel

**la escultura**
la esskooltoo-ra
sculpture

**el triángulo**
el tree-an-goolo
triangle

**el marco**
el marko
frame

**el cubo**
el koobo
cube

**el círculo**
el theer-koolo
circle

**la media luna**
la med-eea loona
crescent

**el cuadrado**
el kwah-drad-o
square

**la paleta**
paleh-ta
palette

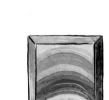

**el arco iris**
el arko eer-iss
rainbow

**el rectángulo**
el rektan-goolo
rectangle

**la esfera**
la essfair-a
sphere

**el cilindro**
el theeleen-dro
cylinder

**la pirámide**
la peeramee-deh
pyramid

**el hexágono**
ex-agono
hexagon

**ovalado/ovalada**
obalad-o/obalad-a
oval

**blanco/blanca**
*blanko/blanka*
white

**negro/negra**
*neg-ro/neg-ra*
black

**azul**
*ah-thool*
blue

**amarillo/amarilla**
*amaree-yo/amaree-ya*
yellow

**marrón**
*mar-on*
brown

**violeta**
*beeo-leta*
violet

**el/la artista**
*el/la arteesta*
artist

**turquesa**
*toorkess-a*
turquoise

**morado/morada**
*morad-o/morad-a*
purple

**rosa**
*rosa*
pink

**rojo/roja**
*ro-ho/ro-ha*
red

**dorado**
*dorad-o*
gold

**plata**
*plah-ta*
silver

**verde**
*bair-deh*
green

**la galería de arte**
*la galairee-a deh arteh*
art gallery

**transparente**
*transpar-en-teh*
transparent

**pálido/pálida**
*pal-eedo/pal-eeda*
pale

**naranja**
*nah-ran-ha*
orange

**multicolor**
*mooltee-kolor*
multicoloured

**gris**
*greess*
greess

39

# El árbol familiar

el *ar*-bol fameelee-*ar*

## Family tree

**el tío abuelo**
el *tee-yo abweh*-lo
great-uncle

**los abuelos**
loss ah-*bweh*-loss
grandparents

**yayo**
*yah*-yo
grandpa
**el abuelo**
el *abweh*-lo
grandfather

**yaya**
*yah*-ya
grandma
**la abuela**
la *abweh*-la
grandmother

**la tía**
la *tee*-ya
aunt

**el tío**
el *tee*-yo
uncle

**los primos/las primas**
loss *pree*-moss/lass *pree*-mass
cousins

**la sobrina**
la soh-*breena*
niece

**el sobrino**
el soh-*breeno*
nephew

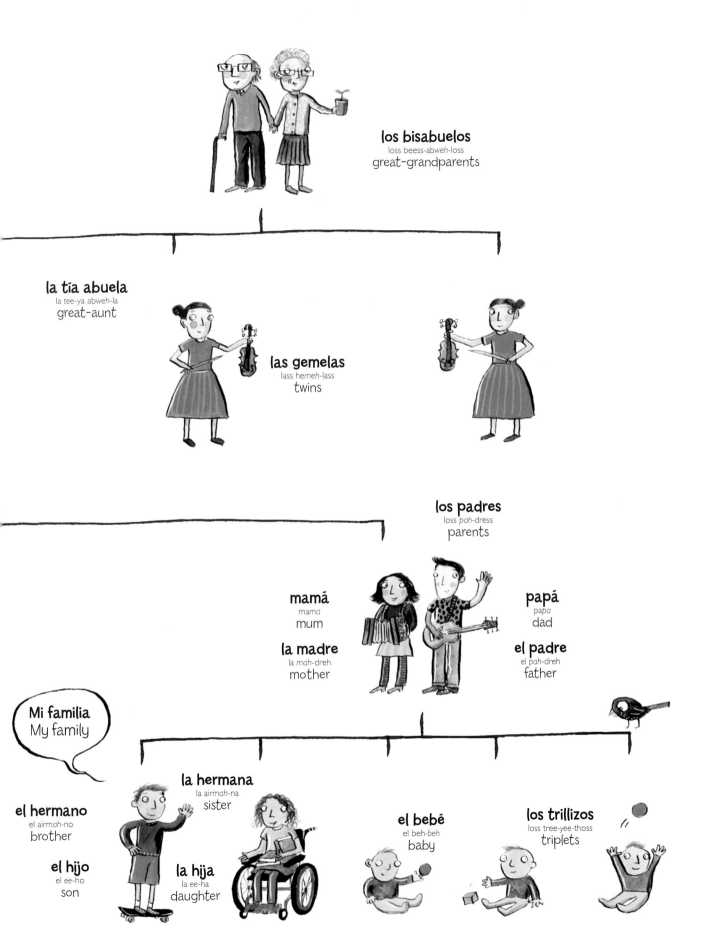

**los bisabuelos**
loss beess-abweh-loss
great-grandparents

**la tía abuela**
la tee-ya abweh-la
great-aunt

**las gemelas**
lass hemeh-lass
twins

**los padres**
loss pah-dress
parents

**mamá**
mama
mum

**la madre**
la mah-dreh
mother

**papá**
papa
dad

**el padre**
el pah-dreh
father

Mi familia
My family

**el hermano**
el airmah-no
brother

**la hermana**
la airmah-na
sister

**el bebé**
el beh-beh
baby

**los trillizos**
loss tree-yee-thoss
triplets

**el hijo**
el ee-ho
son

**la hija**
la ee-ha
daughter

# En el hospital
en el osspee-*tal*
## At the hospital

**el hospital**
el ospee-*tal*
hospital

**el/la cirujano**
el/la theeroo-*hah*-no
surgeon

**los visitantes**
loss beesee-*tan*-tess
visitors

**dolor de barriga**
*dolor* deh baree-ga
tummy ache

**el tubo**
el *toobo*
tube

**la ambulancia**
la amboo-*lan*-thee-a
ambulance

**el quirófano**
el keerof-ano
operating theatre

**el fonendoscopio**
el fonendoss-*kopee*-o
stethoscope

**las pastillas**
lass pastee-yass
tablets

**los puntos**
loss *poontoss*
stitches

**la sala de espera**
la *sah*-la deh es*paira*
waiting-room

**dolor de cabeza**
*dolor* deh k*abeh*-tha
headache

42

**el accidente**
el ak-thee-*denteh*
accident

**la venda**
la *benda*
bandage

**el busca**
el *booss*-ka
bleeper/pager

**el gráfico**
el *graf*-eeko
chart

**los instrumentos**
loss eenstroomen-toss
instruments

**el pasillo**
el passee-yo
corridor

**el doctor/la doctora**
el dok-*tor*/la dok-*tora*
doctor

**el termómetro**
el tair-*mometro*
thermometer

**la máquina de rayos X**
la *makeena* deh *rah*-yoss eeks
x-ray machine

**la inyección**
la een-yek-thee-*on*
injection

**las muletas**
lass moolet-ass
crutches

**la medicina**
la medee-*theena*
medicine

**el enfermero/
la enfermera**
el enfair-*mairo*/la enfair-*maira*
nurse

**el bar**
el bar
snack bar

**el cabestrillo**
el kabess-*tree*-yo
sling

**la tirita**
la tee-ree-tah
plaster

**la operación**
la opairathee-*on*
operation

**dolor de muelas**
dolor deh moo-el-ass
toothache

**la radiografía**
la radeeo-grafeea
x-ray

43

**el mago**
el *mah*-go
magician

# Los oficios
loss o*fee*-theeoss
## Jobs

*There is a different word for many of these jobs depending on whether you are a boy or a girl. They are all in the word list at the back of the book. On this page, you will find the version that goes with the picture.*

**el científico**
el thee-en-*teef*eeko
scientist

**la guarda del zoo**
la goo-*arda* del tho
zookeeper

**el vendedor**
el vended-*or*
sales assistant

**la bailarina**
la bah-eela-reena
dancer

**el cobrador**
el ko*brador*
ticket collector

**el taxista**
el takseesta
taxi-driver

**la secretaria**
la se*kretar*-eea
secretary

**la veterinaria**
la vetaireen-*ar*-eea
vet

**el basurero**
el bassoo-*rairo*
refuse collector

**el cocinero**
el kothee-*nairo*
chef

**la estrella del Pop**
la ess*tray*-a del pop
popstar

**la policía**
la polee-*thee*-a
police officer

**la lampista**
la lam*peesta*
plumber

44

**el panadero**
el pana*dair*-o
baker

**el constructor**
el konstrook-*tor*
builder

**el conductor
de autobús**
el kondook-*tor* deh ah-oto-*boos*
bus driver

**el maquinista**
el makeeneesta
train driver

**la dentista**
la denteesta
dentist

**el electricista**
el elektree-*theess*-ta
electrician

**el carnicero**
el karnee-*thairo*
butcher

**el granjero**
el gran-*hairo*
farmer

**el bombero**
el bom*bair*-o
firefighter

**la auxiliar
de vuelo**
la ah-oox-eelee-*ar*
deh boo-el-o
flight attendant

**el futbolista**
el footbol*eesta*
footballer

**el jardinero**
el hardee*nairo*
gardener

**el piloto**
el peel-oto
pilot

**la camionera**
la kameeon-*aira*
lorry driver

**el salvavidas**
el salba-*beedass*
lifeguard

**el abogado**
el abog*ad*-o
lawyer

**la peluquera**
la pelook*aira*
hairdresser

45

# Los números

Loss *noomaiross*

## How many . . . can you find? ¿Cuántos hay? ¿Puedes descubrirlo?

**20** **veinte**
*vayn-teh*
twenty

**19** **diecinueve**
*dee-eh-thee-noo-eh-beh*
nineteen

**18** **dieciocho**
*dee-eh-thee-ocho*
eighteen

**17** **diecisiete**
*dee-eh-thee-see-eh-teh*
seventeen

**16** **dieciséis**
*dee-eh-thee-sayss*
sixteen

**15** **quince**
*kin-theh*
fifteen

**14** **catorce**
*kat-or-theh*
fourteen

**13** **trece**
*treth-eh*
thirteen

46

 **1** uno/una
*oono/oona*
one

 **2** dos
*doss*
two

 **3** tres
*tress*
three

 **4** cuatro
*kwat-ro*
four

 **5** cinco
*think-o*
five

 **6** seis
*say-ss*
six

 **7** siete
*see-eh-teh*
seven

 **8** ocho
*ocho*
eight

 **9** nueve
*noo-eh-beh*
nine

 **12** doce
*doth-eh*
twelve

**11** once
*on-theh*
eleven

**10** diez
*dee-eth*
ten

47

# Los opuestos

Loss opoo-esstoss

## Opposites

**lento/lenta**
*lento/lenta*
slow

**rápido/rápida**
*rah-peedo/rah-peeda*
fast

**enfadado/enfadada**
*enfadad-o/enfadad-a*
angry

**calmado/calmada**
*kalmad-o/kalmad-a*
calm

**desordenado/
desordenada**
*dess-ordenad-o/dess-ordenad-a*
messy

**ordenado/ordenada**
*ordenad-o/ordenad-a*
tidy

**mojado/mojada**
*mo-had-o/mo-had-a*
wet

**seco/seca**
*sek-o/sek-a*
dry

**ruidoso/ruidosa**
*rooee-doss-o/rooee-doss-a*
noisy

**silencioso/silenciosa**
*seelen-theeoss-o/seelen-theeoss-a*
quiet

**triste**
*treess-teh*
sad

**feliz**
*fel-eeth*
happy

**corto/
corta**
*kor-to/kor-tah*
short

**largo/larga**
*largo/larga*
long

**enfermo/
enferma**
*enfairmo/enfairma*
ill

**sano/
sana**
*sah-no/sah-na*
healthy

48

**malo/mala**
*mah-lo/mah-la*
bad

**bueno/buena**
*bwayno/bwayna*
good

**hermoso/hermosa**
*airmo-so/airmo-sa*
beautiful

**feo/fea**
*fay-o/fay-a*
ugly

**grande**
*gran-deh*
big

**pequeño/pequeña**
*peken-yo/peken-ya*
small

**sucio/sucia**
*soothee-o/soothee-a*
dirty

**limpio/limpia**
*leempeeo/leempeea*
clean

**primero/
primera**
*preemairo/preemaira*
first

**último/última**
*ool-teemo/ool-teema*
last

**viejo/vieja**
*bee-eh-ho/bee-eh-ha*
old

**joven**
*hoven*
young

**ligero/ligera**
*lee-hairo/lee-haira*
light

**diferente**
*deefairen-teh*
different

**igual**
*eegwal*
same

**frío/fría**
*free-o/free-a*
cold

**caliente**
*kalee-enteh*
hot

**vacío/vacía**
*bah-thee-o/bah-thee-a*
empty

**lleno/llena**
*yay-no/yay-na*
full

**pesado/pesada**
*pessah-do/pessah-da*
heavy

**el astronauta**
el astrona-oo-ta
astronaut

# Espacio, tiempo y estaciones
espath-eeo tee-empo ee essta-thee-oness
## Space, weather and seasons

**el extraterrestre**
el ekstra-terrestreh
alien

**el invierno**
el eenbee-yair-no
winter

**el viento**
el bee-ento
wind

**la tormenta**
la tor-men-ta
storm

**el tornado**
el tornad-o
tornado

**el sol**
el sol
sun

**la estrella**
la esstray-a
star

**el verano**
el bairah-no
summer

**el océano**
el othay-ano
ocean

**el transbordador
espacial**
el transbordad-or esspathee-al
space shuttle

**el muñeco de nieve**
el moon-yek-o deh nee-eh-beh
snowman

**la nieve**
la nee-eh-beh
snow

**el cielo**
el thee-aylo
sky

**el asteroide**
el astero-eedeh
asteroid

**el OVNI**
el ov-nee
UFO

**el continente**
el konteenen-teh
continent

**la nube**
la noo-beh
cloud

**el cometa**
el komay-ta
comet

**el otoño**
el oton-yo
autumn

**la Tierra**
la tee-aira
Earth

**la niebla**
la nee-aybla
fog

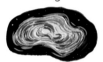

**la galaxia**
la galakseea
galaxy

**el granizo**
el graneetho
hail

**el hielo**
el ee-aylo
ice

**el relámpago**
el rel-lam-pago
lightning

**la luna**
la loona
moon

**el satélite**
el satel-eeteh
satellite

**el cohete**
el kweteh
rocket

**la lluvia**
la yoo-beea
rain

**la órbita**
la or-beeta
orbit

**los planetas**
loss planet-ass
planets

**la primavera**
la preema-vaira
spring

51

# La ropa

la *ropa*

## Clothes

**el bolso de señora**
el *bolsso* deh *senyor*-a
handbag

**el reloj**
el *relok*
watch

**la pulsera**
la pool-*saira*
bracelet

**la camisa**
la *kam-ee-sa*
shirt

**el pantalón**
el *pantalon*
trousers

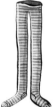

**las medias**
las *med-eeass*
tights

**la camiseta**
la *kamee-say-ta*
T-shirt

**el pijama**
el *peehah*-ma
pyjamas

**las zapatillas**
lass *thapatee-yass*
slippers

**los pantalones cortos**
loss *panta-loness* *kor-toss*
shorts

**el cinturón**
el *theen-too-ron*
belt

**la bufanda**
la *boofan*-da
scarf

**los calcetines**
loss *kaltheh-tee-ness*
socks

**el chaleco**
el *chalay*-ko
waistcoat

**las sandalias**
lass *sandalee-ass*
sandals

**el anillo**
el *anee-yo*
ring

**los zapatos**
los *thapat*-toss
shoes

**el poncho**
el *poncho*
poncho

**las botas**
las *botass*
boots

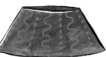

**la falda**
la *fal*-da
skirt

**la gorra**
la *gor*-a
cap

**la rebeca**
la reh-beka
cardigan

**la mochila**
la moh-*cheelah*
bag

**el vestido**
el *besteedo*
dress

**las botas
de fútbol**
lass *botass* deh *foot*-bol
football boots

**las gafas**
lass *gafass*
glasses

**los guantes**
loss *gwan*-tess
gloves

**el abrigo**
el *abree*-go
coat

**la chaqueta**
la *chakay*-ta
jacket

**el sombrero**
el *sombrairo*
hat

**el suéter**
el *swet*-air
jumper

**el maquillaje**
el makee-*yah*-heh
make-up

**el bolsillo**
el bolsee-yo
pocket

**los calzoncillos**
loss calthon-seeyos
pants

**el vestido de noche**
el bes-*teed*-o deh *nocheh*
nightdress

**el collar**
el *koyar*
necklace

**el esmalte de uñas**
el ess*mal*-teh deh *oonass*
nail varnish

# Palabras adicionales

pah-*lah*-brass adeeth-eeon*ah*-les

## Additional words

Here are some words that you will find useful as you practise your Spanish at home.
They did not make it into the illustrated scenes in the book so they are gathered here for reference.
These words also appear in the word lists at the back of the book.

| | | | | | |
|---|---|---|---|---|---|
| **izquierdo/ izquierda** <br> eeth-*kaird*-o/eeth-*kaird*-a <br> left | **derecho/ derecha** <br> dair-ech-o/dair-ech-a <br> right | **delante de** <br> delan-teh deh <br> in front of | **Sra.** <br> sen-*yora* <br> Mrs. | **Sr.** <br> sen-*yor* <br> Mr. | **el nombre** <br> el *nom*-breh <br> name |
| **mí** <br> mee <br> me | **tú** <br> too <br> you | **ella** <br> eh-ya <br> she | **ella** <br> eh-ya <br> her | **él** <br> el <br> he | **le** <br> leh <br> him |
| **enero** <br> en-airo <br> January | **febrero** <br> feb-rairo <br> February | **marzo** <br> martho <br> March | **abril** <br> abreel <br> April | **mayo** <br> mah-yo <br> May | **junio** <br> hoon-yo <br> June |
| **julio** <br> hool-yo <br> July | **agosto** <br> ah-gos-to <br> August | **septiembre** <br> sept-*yem*-breh <br> September | **octubre** <br> ok-*too* breh <br> October | **noviembre** <br> nob-yem-breh <br> November | **diciembre** <br> deeth-*yem*-breh <br> December |
| **lunes** <br> loo-ness <br> Monday | **martes** <br> mar-tess <br> Tuesday | **miércoles** <br> mee-air-koless <br> Wednesday | **jueves** <br> hoo-*ah*-bess <br> Thursday | **viernes** <br> bee-*air*-ness <br> Friday | **sábado** <br> sab-ad-o <br> Saturday |
| **domingo** <br> dom-eengo <br> Sunday | **hoy** <br> oy <br> today | **ayer** <br> ah-ee-*air* <br> yesterday | **mañana** <br> manyana <br> morning | **la tarde** <br> la *tar*-deh <br> afternoon | **noche** <br> noch-eh <br> night |
| **los dias** <br> lass dee-ass <br> days | **los meses** <br> loss meh-says <br> months | **el año** <br> el an-yo <br> year | **el cumpleaños** <br> el komplay-an-yos <br> birthday | **cien** <br> thee-en <br> hundred | **mil** <br> meel <br> thousand |
| **brillante** <br> bree-yan-teh <br> bright | **vívido/vívida** <br> beebeed-o/beebeed-a <br> vivid | **oscuro** <br> oss-kooro <br> dark | **la competencia** <br> la kompet-enthee-a <br> competition | **el viaje** <br> el bee-ahay <br> travel | **la altura** <br> la al-toor-ah <br> height |
| **en/sobre** <br> en/sobreh <br> on | **detrás** <br> det-rass <br> behind | **bajo** <br> bah-ho <br> under | **un abrazo** <br> oon ah-brathoh <br> hug | **un beso** <br> oon beso <br> kiss | **el peso** <br> el *peso* <br> weight |

## A note about boys and girls:

Many of the Spanish words describing jobs or people have both a masculine and feminine version. It is similar to the difference in English between 'actor' and 'actress'. Both words have been included separately in the word list with an '(m)' for masculine and '(f)' for feminine after them. Not all of the words follow this pattern. If you are not sure, look up the English word to check. Adjectives also come in two versions with the masculine version first followed by the feminine version. More often than not, the masculine word ends in 'o' and the feminine word ends in 'a'. But this isn't always the case so make sure you check.

# Lista de palabras Word list

## Spanish/español - English/inglés

la abogada  lawyer (f)
el abogado  lawyer (m)
abrazar  hugging
abrazo  hug
el abrigo  coat
abril  April
la abuela  grandmother
el abuelo  grandfather
los abuelos  grandparents
el acantilado  cliff
el accidente  accident
la acera  pavement
acostarse  going to sleep
los aerobics  aerobics
el aeropuerto  airport
agosto  August
el agua  water
la alacena  cupboard
el alfabeto  alphabet
la alfombra  rug
la alfombrilla  mat
el alga marina  seaweed
el algodón de azúcar
  candyfloss
la almohada  pillow
los altavoces  speakers
la altura  height
la alumna  pupil (f)
el alumno  pupil (m)
amarillo/amarilla  yellow
la ambulancia  ambulance
la amiga  friend (f)
el amigo  friend (m)
las amigas  friends (f)
los amigos  friends (m)
el andamio  scaffolding
andar  walking
el andén  platform
el anillo  ring
los animales  animals
el año  year
el aparador  dresser
el apartamento  apartment
el apio  celery
la araña  spider
el/la árbitro  referee (m/f)
el árbol  tree
el árbol familiar  family tree
el arco iris  rainbow
la ardilla  squirrel
la arena  sand

el armario  wardrobe
el arroyo  stream
el arroz  rice
el/la artista  artist (m/f)
el ascensor  lift
el asiento  seat
el aspirador  vacuum cleaner
el asteroide  asteroid
el astronauta  astronaut
el atletismo  athletics
los auriculares  headphones
el autobús  bus
el/la auxiliar de vuelo  flight
  attendant (m/f)
el aviario  aviary
el avión  aeroplane
ayer  yesterday
azul  blue
el babero  bib
el badminton  badminton
bailar  dancing
el bailarín  dancer (m)
la bailarina  dancer (f)
bajo  under
el balancín  see-saw
la ballena  whale
el balón de fútbol  football
el baloncesto  basketball
el banco  bank
el banco  bench
la bandera  flag
la bañera  bath
el baño  bathroom
el bar  snack bar
la barbilla  chin
el barco  boat
el barco  ship
el barco de pesca  fishing boat
la barriga  tummy
el bastón  walking stick
la basurera  refuse collector (f)
el basurero  refuse collector (m)
el baúl  trunk
el bebé  baby
el bebedero  trough
beber  drinking
la berenjena  aubergine
besar  kissing
beso  kiss
la biblioteca  library
la bicicleta  bicycle

el billete  ticket
los bisabuelos
  great-grandparents
blanco/blanca  white
los bloques  blocks
la boca  mouth
el bocadillo  sandwich
la bolsa de la compra
  shopping bag
la bolsa de deporte  sports
bag
la bolsa del cartero  postbag
el bolsillo  pocket
el bolso de señora  handbag
el bombero  firefighter (m)
la bombero  firefighter (f)
el bosque  forest
las botas  boots
las botas  walking boots
las botas de agua
  wellington boots
las botas de fútbol
  football boots
el bote  dinghy
el bote a remos  rowing boat
la botella  bottle
la boya  buoy
el brazo  arm
brillante  bright
la bruja  witch
el buceador  diver (m)
la buceadora  diver (f)
bueno/buena  good
la bufanda  scarf
el buho  owl
el bulldozer  bulldozer
el busca  bleeper/pager
el buzón  postbox
el caballero  knight
el caballete  easel
el caballito balancín
  rocking horse
el caballo  horse
el cabestrillo  sling
la cabeza  head
la cabra  goat
el cabrito  kid
  (baby goat)
la cacerola  saucepan
el cachorro  puppy
el cactus  cactus

el café  café
el café  coffee
la caja de herramientas
  toolbox
la caja registradora  till
el cajón de arena  sandpit
el calabacín  courgette
los calcetines  socks
caliente  hot
calmado/calmada  calm
los calzoncillos  pants
la cama  bed
el camaleón  chameleon
el camino  path
el camión  lorry
el camión hormigonera
  cement mixer
la camionera  lorry driver (f)
el camionero  lorry driver (m)
la camisa  shirt
la camiseta  T-shirt
el campamento  campsite
el campo  countryside
la cancha de tenis  tennis
court
el cangrejo  crab
el canguro  kangaroo
cantar  singing
la capa  cloak
la cara  face
el caracol  snail
la carnicería  butcher's
la carnicera  butcher (f)
el carnicero  butcher (m)
la carrera  race
la carretera  road
la carretilla  wheelbarrow
el carrito  pushchair
el carrito  trolley
la carta  letter
el cartel  signpost
la cartera  satchel
el cartero  postman
la casa  home
la casa  house
la casa de muñecas  doll's
house
la cascada  waterfall
la casita del árbol  treehouse
el castillo  castle
el castillo de arena  sandcastle

# Spanish/español - English/inglés

el **castor** beaver
**catorce** fourteen
la **cebolla** onion
la **cebra** zebra
el **centro deportivo** sports centre
el **cepillo de dientes** toothbrush
el **cepillo del pelo** hairbrush
el **cerdito** piglet
el **cerdo** pig
el **cereal** cereal
el **cerebro** brain
la **cereza** cherry
el **césped** lawn
la **cesta** basket
el **chaleco** waistcoat
el **chaleco salvavidas** life jacket
el **champú** shampoo
la **chaqueta** jacket
el **chocolate** chocolate
el **cielo** sky
**cien** hundred
la **científica** scientist (f)
el **científico** scientist (m)
el **ciervo** deer
el **cilindro** cylinder
**cinco** five
el **cine** cinema
el **cinturón** belt
el **círculo** circle
el/la **cirujano** surgeon
el **cisne** swan
el **cisne pequeñito** cygnet
la **cisterna pluvial** water butt
la **ciudad** town
la **clase** classroom
el **clavo** nail
el **cobertizo** shed
el **cobrador** ticket collector (m)
la **cobradora** ticket collector (f)
el **coche** car
el **coche de bomberos** fire engine
el **coche de policía** police car
la **cocina** cooker
la **cocina** kitchen
**cocinar** cooking
la **cocinera** chef (f)
el **cocinero** chef (m)
el **cocodrilo** crocodile
el **codo** elbow
el **cohete** rocket
el **cojín** cushion
la **col** cabbage

la **colcha** duvet
la **colina** hill
el **collar** necklace
el **collar de cuentas** beads
los **colores** colours
el **columpio** swing
el **comedero de pájaros** bird feeder
el **comedor** dining room
**comer** eating
el **cometa** comet
la **cometa** kite
la **comida** food
la **comida** meal
la **cómoda** chest of drawers
la **competición** competition
el **compost** compost heap
la **concha** shell
el **conductor de autobús** bus driver (m)
la **conductora de autobús** bus driver (f)
el **conejo** rabbit
la **constructora** builder (f)
el **constructor** builder (m)
el **continente** continent
el **coral** coral
el **corazón** heart
el **cordero** lamb
la **corona** crown
el **corredor** jogger (m)
la **corredora** jogger (f)
**correr** running
el **cortacésped** lawnmower
las **cortinas** curtains
**corto/corta** short
la **cosechadora** combine harvester
el **cráneo** skull
el **cuadrado** square
el **cuadro** painting
el **cuadro** picture
**cuatro** four
el **cubo** bucket
el **cubo** cube
la **cuchara** spoon
el **cuchillo** knife
el **cuello** neck
la **cuerda** rope
la **cuerda de saltar** skipping rope
el **cuerpo** body
el **cuervo** crow
el **cumpleaños** birthday
la **cuna** cot

los **dados** dice
**dar volteretas** doing somersaults
el **dedo** finger
el **dedo del pie** toe
el **delantal** apron
**delante de** in front of
el **delfín** dolphin
el/la **dentista** dentist
los **deportes** sport
**derecho/derecha** right
el **desayuno** breakfast
**desordenado/desordenada** messy
el **despertador** alarm clock
**detrás** behind
el **dia festivo** holiday
las **días** days
**dibujar** drawing
el **diccionario** dictionary
**diciembre** December
**diecinueve** nineteen
**dieciocho** eighteen
**dieciséis** sixteen
**diecisiete** seventeen
los **dientes** teeth
**diez** ten
**diferente** different
el **dinero** money
el **director** head teacher (f)
la **directora** head teacher (f)
el **disfraz de superhéroe** superhero costume
**doce** twelve
el **doctor** doctor (m)
la **doctora** doctor (f)
**dolor de barriga** tummy ache
**dolor de cabeza** headache
**dolor de muelas** toothache
**domingo** Sunday
el **dominó** dominoes
**dorado** gold
el **dormitorio** bedroom
**dos** two
el **dragón** dragon
la **ducha** shower
el **dúmper** dumper truck
el **DVD** DVD
**él** he
el/la **electricista** electrician (m/f)
el **elefante** elephant
**ella** her
**ella** she
**empujar** pushing

**en/sobre** on
**enero** January
**enfadado/enfadada** angry
la **enfermera** nurse (f)
el **enfermero** nurse (m)
**enfermo/enferma** ill
la **ensalada** salad
el **entrenador** coach (m)
la **entrenadora** coach (f)
el **equipaje** luggage
el **equipo** team
el **equipo de deporte** sports kit
**escalar** climbing
la **escalera** ladder
la **escalera mecánica** escalator
el **escarabajo** beetle
la **escoba** broom
**escribir** writing
la **escuela** school
la **escultura** sculpture
la **esfera** sphere
el **esmalte de uñas** nail varnish
el **espacio** space
la **espalda** back
el **espantapájaros** scarecrow
el **espejo** mirror
la **esponja** sponge
el **esqueleto** skeleton
**esquiar** skiing los **esquís** skis
la **estación de tren** rail station
las **estaciones** seasons
el **estanque** pond
la **estantería** bookshelf
la **estantería** shelf
**estar de pie** standing
**estar sentado** sitting
la **estrella de mar** starfish
la **estrella del Pop** popstar
la **estrella** star
la **excavadora** digger
el **extraterrestre** alien
la **fábrica** factory
la **falda** skirt
la **familia** family
el **fango** mud
la **farmacia** chemist
el **faro** lighthouse
**febrero** February

# Spanish/español – English/inglés

feliz happy
feo/fea ugly
el ferry ferry
la fiesta party
la flauta recorder
la flor flower
el florero vase
el fondo del mar under the sea
el fonendoscopio stethoscope
las formas shapes
el fregadero sink
la fresa strawberry
el frigorífico fridge
frío/fría cold
la fruta fruit
el fuego fire
la furgoneta van
el futbolín table football
el/la futbolista footballer (m/f)
las gafas glasses
las gafas de natación goggles
las gafas de sol sunglasses
la galaxia galaxy
la galería de arte art gallery
las galletas biscuits
la gallina chicken
el ganso goose
el garaje garage
la gasolinera petrol station
gatear crawling
el gatito kitten
el gato cat
la gaviota seagull
las gemelas twins (f)
los gemelos twins (m)
el genio genie
el gigante giant
la gimnasia gymnastics
el globo balloon
el globo terráqueo globe
la goma de borrar rubber
la glorieta pavilion
el gorila gorilla
la gorra cap
el gráfico chart
grande big
el granero barn
el granizo hail
la granja farm
la granja farmhouse
la granjera farmer (f)

el granjero farmer (m)
gris grey
la grulla crane
los guantes gloves
el/la guarda del zoo zookeeper (m/f)
la guitarra guitar
hablar talking
hacer el pino doing a handstand
hacer la rueda doing a cartwheel
el hacha axe
el hada fairy
el hámster hamster
el helado ice-cream
el helicóptero helicopter
el heno hay
la hermana sister
el hermano brother
hermoso/hermosa beautiful
el hexágono hexagon
el hielo ice
la hierba grass
la hija daughter
el hijo son
el hipopótamo hippopotamus
la hoja leaf
los hombros shoulders
el hospital hospital
el hotel hotel
hoy today
el huerto garden
el huerto orchard
el huerto vegetable garden
el hueso bone
la huevera egg cup
los huevos eggs
igual same
los instrumentos instruments
el invernadero greenhouse
el invierno winter
la inyección injection
izquierdo/izquierda left
el jabón soap
el jamón ham
la jardinera gardener (f)
el jardinero gardener (m)
el jardinero park-keeper
la jarra de agua jug of water
la jaula cage
la jirafa giraffe
joven young
el joyero jewellery box
el juego game

el juego de magia magic set
jueves Thursday
jugar playing
los juguetes toys
julio July
la jungla jungle
junio June
el kiwi kiwi
el koala koala
el labio lip
el ladrillo brick
el lagarto lizard
el lago lake
la lámpara desk lamp
la lámpara lamp
la lámpara mágica magic lamp
el/la lampista plumber (m/f)
la langosta lobster
los lápices de colores coloured pencils
el lápiz pencil
largo/larga long
el lavabo washbasin
la lavadora washing machine
lavar los dientes cleaning your teeth
la vajilla sucia washing-up
lavarse having a wash
le him
la leche milk
la lechuga lettuce
leer reading
la lengua tongue
lento/lenta slow
el león lion
levantarse getting up
el libro book
el libro de cuentos storybook
el libro de texto textbook
ligero/ligera light
la limonada lemonade
el limón lemon
limpio/limpia clean
la llave key
lleno/llena full
llevar carrying
la lluvia rain
el lobo wolf
la loción solar suncream
la lombriz worm
el loro parrot
la luna moon
lunes Monday
la maceta plant pot

la madera wood
la madre mother
la madriguera burrow
la madriguera del ratón mouse hole
las magdalenas cupcakes
el/la mago magician (m/f)
el maíz corn
la maleta suitcase
malo/mala bad
mamá mum
la mañana morning
las manchas stains
el mando a distancia remote control
el mango mango
la manguera hose
la mano hand
la manta blanket
la mantequilla butter
la manzana apple
el manzano apple tree
el mapa map
el mapache racoon
la maqueta de avión model aeroplane
el maquillaje make-up
la máquina de rayos X x-ray machine
el/la maquinista train driver (m/f)
el marcador scoreboard
el marco frame
la mariposa butterfly
marrón brown
martes Tuesday
el martillo hammer
marzo March
el matasuegras party blower
el matorral bush
mayo May
la media luna crescent
las medias tights
la medicina medicine
la medusa jellyfish
la mejilla cheek
el melocotón peach
el mercado market
la merienda snack
la mermelada jam
la mesa table
los meses months
la mesita de noche bedside table

# Spanish/español – English/inglés

mí me

miércoles Wednesday

mil thousand

el minigolf mini-golf

la mochila bag

la mochila rucksack

mojado/mojada wet

el monedero purse

el mono monkey

la montaña mountain

montar en bicicleta cycling

morado/morada purple

la morsa walrus

la mosca fly

el mosquito mosquito

la motocicleta motorbike

la mountain bike mountain bike

el móvil mobile phone

los muebles furniture

las muletas crutches

multicolor multicoloured

la muñeca doll

el muñeco de nieve snowman

el murciélago bat

el muro wall

el museo museum

la música music

nadar swimming

la naranja orange (fruit)

naranja orange (colour)

la nariz nose

el naufragio wreck

negro/negra black

la niebla fog

la nieve snow

la niña girl

el niño boy

el niño/la niña child (m/f)

el noche night

el nombre name

noviembre November

la nube cloud

nueve nine

los números numbers

la nutria otter

la obra building site

el océano ocean

ocho eight

octubre October

la oficina office

la oficina de correos post office

los oficios jobs

los ojos eyes

la ola wave

once eleven

la operación operation

los opuestos opposites

la órbita orbit

ordenado/ordenada tidy

el ordenador computer

la oreja ear

la oruga caterpillar

oscuro dark

el osito de peluche teddy bear

el oso pardo brown bear

el oso pardo grizzly bear

el oso polar polar bear

el otoño autumn

ovalado/ovalada oval

la oveja sheep

el OVNI UFO

el padre father

los padres parents

el pájaro bird

la pala spade

la paleta trowel

la paleta palette

pálido/pálida pale

el palo stick

el palomo pigeon

palos para trepar climbing frame

el pan bread

la panadería bakery

la panadera baker (f)

el panadero baker (m)

el panal beehive

el panda panda

el paño de cocina tea towel

la pantalla lampshade

el pantalón trousers

los pantalones cortos shorts

los pañuelos tissues

el papá dad

el papel paper

la papelera bin

el papel higiénico toilet paper

la parada del bus bus stop

el paraguas umbrella

el parque park

el parque infantil playground

el partido de fútbol football match

el pasillo corridor

el paso a nivel level crossing

el paso de peatones pedestrian crossing

la pasta pasta

la pasta de dientes toothpaste

el pastel cake

las pastillas tablets

el pastor shepherd

la patata potato

las patatas fritas chips

los patines rollerblades

el patio yard

el patito duckling

el pato duck

el pecho chest

el pegamento glue

el peine comb

el pelo hair

la pelota ball

la pelota de playa beach ball

los peluches cuddly toys

la peluquera hairdresser (f)

el peluquero hairdresser (m)

el pepino cucumber

pequeño/pequeña small

la pera pear

el perro dog

el perro pastor sheepdog

pesado/pesada heavy

el pescado fish (to eat)

pescar fishing

el peso weight

el pez fish (in water)

el picnic picnic

el pie foot

las piedras stones

la pierna leg

el pijama pyjamas

el/la piloto pilot (m/f)

la piña pineapple

el pincel paintbrush

el ping pong table tennis

el pingüino penguin

pintar painting

las pinturas paints

la piragua canoe

la pirámide pyramid

el pirata pirate

la piruleta lollipop

la piscina swimming-pool

la piscina de niños paddling pool

la pizarra whiteboard

la pizza pizza

los planetas planets

la planta plant

plata silver

el plátano banana

el platillo saucer

los platillos cymbals

el plato plate

la playa beach

la pluma feather

la pluma pen

el/la policía police officer (m/f)

el pollito chick

el pollo chicken (to eat)

el poncho poncho

el pony pony

el portacontenedores container ship

el portátil laptop

el portero goalkeeper

el posavasos coaster

el póster poster

el potro foal

el prado field

la primavera spring

primero/primera first

las primas cousins (f)

los primos cousins (m)

la princesa princess

el príncipe prince

los prismáticos binoculars

el profesor teacher (m)

la profesora teacher (f)

el puente bridge

la puerta door

la puerta de la verja gate

el puerto port

los pulmones lungs

el pulpo octopus

la pulsera bracelet

los puntos stitches

el pupitre desk

el quad quadbike

el queso cheese

quince fifteen

el quirófano operating theatre

la radio radio

la radiografía x-ray

los raíles rails

la rama branch

la rana frog

rápido/rápida fast

la raqueta racket

el rastrillo rake

la rata rat

el ratón mouse

la rebeca cardigan

# Spanish/español - English/inglés

el rectángulo rectangle
el refresco cola
el refugio shelter
la regadera watering-can
el regalo present
la regla ruler
la reina queen
el relámpago lightning
el reloj clock
el reloj watch
el remo oar
el remo paddle
el remolque trailer
el renacuajo tadpole
el reno reindeer
el reposapiés footstool
el restaurante restaurant
el retrete toilet
el rey king
el rincón de lectura reading corner
el rinoceronte rhinocero
el río river
el robot robot
la roca rock
la rodilla knee
rojo/roja red
el rompecabezas jigsaw
la ropa clothes
rosa pink
la rotonda roundabout
ruidoso/ruidosa noisy
sábado Saturday
la sábana sheet
el saco sack
la sala de espera waiting-room
las salchichas sausages
el salón sitting room
saltar jumping
el salto de altura high jump
el salto de longitud long jump
el salvavidas rubber ring
el/la salvavidas lifeguard (m/f)
las sandalias sandals
sano/sana healthy
el satélite satellite
la sauna sauna
seco/seca dry
la secretaria secretary
seis six
el semáforo traffic lights
la señal signal
la señal de tráfico road sign
señalar pointing
el sendero track

septiembre September
la serpentina streamer
la serpiente snake
el serrucho saw
la servilleta napkin
el seto hedge
siete seven
el silbato whistle
la silla de ruedas wheelchair
silencioso/silenciosa quiet
la silla chair
el sillón armchair
la sirena mermaid
la sobrina niece
el sobrino nephew
el sofá sofa
el sol sun
el sombrero hat
el sombrero de fiesta party hat
la sombrilla beach umbrella
Sr. Mr.
Sra. Mrs.
sucio/sucia dirty
el suelo floor
el suéter jumper
el supermercado supermarket
el/la surfista surfer (m/f)
el suricato meerkat
la tabla de surf surfboard
la tablet tablet
el taburete stool
la tacita beaker
el taco de salida starting block
el tambor drum
la tarde afternoon
el/la taxista taxi-driver (m/f)
la taza cup
el tazón bowl
el té tea
el techo ceiling
el tejón badger
el teléfono telephone
la televisión television
el tenderete stall
el tenedor fork
el tenis tennis
el termómetro thermometer
el ternero calf
la tetera teapot
la tía aunt
la tía abuela great-aunt
la tiara tiara
el tiburón shark
el tiempo weather
la tienda shop

la tienda de campaña tent
la tienda de juguetes toyshop
la tienda de mascotas petshop
la tienda de libros bookshop
la Tierra Earth
el tigre tiger
las tijeras scissors
el tío uncle
el tío abuelo great-uncle
tirar pulling
la tirita plaster
los títeres puppets
la toalla towel
el tobillo ankle
el tobogán slide
el tomate tomato
la tormenta storm
el tornado tornado
la tostada toast
el tractor tractor
el traje de baño swimming costume
el trampolín diving board
el transbordador espacial space shuttle
transparente transparent
el transporte transport
trece thirteen
el tren train
el trenecito de juguete toy train
tres three
el triángulo triangle
el triciclo tricycle
el trigo wheat
los trillizos triplets
triste sad
la trompeta trumpet
la trona highchair
el tronco log
tú you
el tubo tube
la tumbona deckchair
el túnel tunnel
turquesa turquoise
último/última last
las uñas nails
uno/una one
las uvas grapes
la vaca cow
vacío/vacía empty
la valla fence

la varita mágica magic wand
el vaso glass
el váter público toilets
los vehículos vehicles
veinte twenty
la vela candle
el velero yacht
la venda bandage
el vendedor sales assistant (m)
la vendedora sales assistant (f)
la ventana window
ver la tele watching TV
el verano summer
verde green
las verduras vegetables
el vestido dress
el vestido de fiesta party dress
el vestido de noche nightdress
el vestuario changing-room
la veterinaria vet (f)
el veterinario vet (m)
el viaje travel
viejo/vieja old
el viento wind
viernes Friday
la viña vineyard
violeta violet
el violín violin
los visitantes visitors
vívido/vívida vivid
el volante shuttlecock
el wok wok
el xilófono xylophone
la yaya grandma
el yayo grandpa
el yoga yoga
el yogur yogurt
la zanahoria carrot
los zancos stilts
las zapatillas de ballet ballet shoes
las zapatillas slippers
los zapatos shoes
el zoo zoo
el zorro fox
el zumo de fruta fruit juice
el zumo de naranja orange juice

# English/inglés – Spanish/español

**accident** el accidente
**aerobics** los aerobics
**aeroplane** el avión
**afternoon** la tarde
**airport** el aeropuerto
**alarm clock** el despertador
**alien** el extraterrestre
**alphabet** el alfabeto
**ambulance** la ambulancia
**angry** enfadado/enfadada
**animals** los animales
**ankle** el tobillo
**apartment** el apartamento
**apple** la manzana
**apple tree** el manzano
**April** abril
**apron** el delantal
**arm** el brazo
**armchair** el sillón
**art gallery** la galería de arte
**artist** el/la artista (m/f)
**asteroid** el asteroide
**astronaut** el astronauta
**athletics** el atletismo
**aubergine** la berenjena
**August** agosto
**aunt** la tía
**autumn** el otoño
**aviary** el aviario
**axe** el hacha
**baby** el bebé
**back** la espalda
**bad** malo/mala
**badger** el tejón
**badminton** el badminton
**bag** la mochila
**baker** el panadero
**bakery** la panadería
**ball** la pelota
**ballet shoes** las zapatillas
  de ballet
**balloon** el globo
**banana** el plátano
**bandage** la venda
**bank** el banco
**barn** el granero
**basket** la cesta
**basketball** el baloncesto
**bat** el murciélago
**bath** la bañera
**bathroom** el baño
**beach** la playa
**beach ball** la pelota de playa
**beach umbrella** la sombrilla
**beads** el collar de cuentas

**beaker** la tacita
**beautiful** hermoso/hermosa
**beaver** el castor
**bed** la cama
**bedroom** el dormitorio
**bedside table** la mesita
  de noche
**beehive** el panal
**beetle** el escarabajo
**behind** detrás
**belt** el cinturón
**bench** el banco
**bib** el babero
**bicycle** la bicicleta
**big** grande
**bin** la papelera
**binoculars** los prismáticos
**bird** el pájaro
**bird feeder** el comedero
  de pájaros
**birthday** el cumpleaños
**biscuits** las galletas
**black** negro/negra
**blanket** la manta
**bleeper/pager** el busca
**blocks** los bloques
**blue** azul
**boat** el barco
**body** el cuerpo
**bone** el hueso
**book** el libro
**bookshelf** la estantería
**bookshop** la tienda de libros
**boots** las botas
**bottle** la botella
**bowl** el tazón
**boy** el niño
**bracelet** la pulsera
**brain** el cerebro
**branch** la rama
**bread** el pan
**breakfast** el desayuno
**brick** el ladrillo
**bridge** el puente
**bright** brillante
**broom** la escoba
**brother** el hermano
**brown** marrón
**brown bear** el oso pardo
**bucket** el cubo
**builder** el constructor
**building site** la obra
**bulldozer** el bulldozer
**buoy** la boya
**burrow** la madriguera

**bus** el autobús
**bus driver** el conductor
  de autobús (m)
**bus driver** la conductora de
  autobús (f)
**bus stop** la parada del bus
**bush** el matorral
**butcher** la carnicera (f)
**butcher** el carnicero (m)
**butcher's** la carnicería
**butter** la mantequilla
**butterfly** la mariposa
**cabbage** la col
**cactus** el cactus
**café** el café
**cage** la jaula
**cake** el pastel
**calf** el ternero
**calm** calmado/calmada
**campsite** el campamento
**candle** la vela
**candyfloss** el algodón
  de azúcar
**canoe** la piragua
**cap** la gorra
**car** el coche
**cardigan** la rebeca
**carrot** la zanahoria
**carrying** llevar
**castle** el castillo
**cat** el gato
**caterpillar** la oruga
**ceiling** el techo
**celery** el apio
**cement mixer** el camión
  hormigonera
**cereal** el cereal
**chair** la silla
**chameleon** el camaleón
**changing-room** el vestuario
**chart** el gráfico
**cheek** la mejilla
**cheese** el queso
**chef** la cocinera
**chef** el cocinero
**chemist** la farmacia
**cherry** la cereza
**chest** el pecho
**chest of drawers** la cómoda
**chick** el pollito
**chicken** la gallina
**chicken (to eat)** el pollo
**child** el niño/la niña
**chin** la barbilla
**chips** las patatas fritas

**chocolate** el chocolate
**cinema** el cine
**circle** el círculo
**classroom** la clase
**clean** limpio/limpia
**cleaning your teeth** lavar
  los dientes
**cliff** el acantilado
**climbing** escalar
**climbing frame** palos
  para trepar
**cloak** la capa
**clock** el reloj
**clothes** la ropa
**cloud** la nube
**coach** el entrenador (m)
**coach** la entrenadora (f)
**coaster** el posavasos
**coat** el abrigo
**coffee** el café
**cola** el refresco
**cold** frío/fría
**coloured pencils**
  los lápices de colores
**colours** los colores
**comb** el peine
**combine harvester**
  la cosechadora
**comet** el cometa
**competition** la competición
**compost heap** el compost
**computer** el ordenador
**container ship**
  el portacontenedores
**continent** el continente
**cooker** la cocina
**cooking** cocinar
**coral** el coral
**corn** el maíz
**corridor** el pasillo
**cot** la cuna
**countryside** el campo
**courgette** el calabacín
**cousins** las primas (f)
**cousins** los primos (m)
**cow** la vaca
**crab** el cangrejo
**crane** la grulla
**crawling** gatear
**crescent** la media luna
**crocodile** el cocodrilo
**crow** el cuervo
**crown** la corona
**crutches** las muletas
**cube** el cubo

# English/inglés – Spanish/español

cucumber el pepino
cuddly toys los peluches
cup la taza
cupboard la alacena
cupcakes las magdalenas
curtains las cortinas
cushion el cojín
cycling montar en bicicleta
cygnet el cisne pequeñito
cylinder el cilindro
cymbals los platillos
dad el papá
dancer el bailarín (m)
dancer la bailarina (f)
dancing bailar
dark oscuro
daughter la hija
days las días
December diciembre
deckchair la tumbona
deer el ciervo
dentist el/la dentista (m/f)
desk el pupitre
desk lamp la lámpara
dice los dados
dictionary el diccionario
different diferente
digger la excavadora
dinghy el bote
dining room el comedor
dirty sucio/sucia
diver el buceador (m)
diver la buceadora (f)
diving board el trampolín
doctor el doctor (m)
doctor la doctora (f)
dog el perro
doing a cartwheel hacer
  la rueda
doing a handstand hacer
  el pino
doing somersaults dar
  volteretas
doll la muñeca
doll's house la casa de
  muñecas
dolphin el delfín
dominoes el dominó
door la puerta
dragon el dragón
drawing dibujar
dress el vestido
dresser el aparador
drinking beber
drum el tambor

dry seco/seca
duck el pato
duckling el patito
dumper truck el dúmper
duvet la colcha
DVD el DVD
ear la oreja
Earth la Tierra
easel el caballete
eating comer
egg cup la huevera
eggs los huevos
eight ocho
eighteen dieciocho
elbow el codo
electrician
  el/la electricista (m/f)
elephant el elefante
eleven once
empty vacío/vacía
escalator la escalera mecánica
eyes los ojos
face la cara
factory la fábrica
fairy el hada
family la familia
family tree el árbol familiar
farm la granja
farmer la granjera (f)
farmer el granjero (m)
farmhouse la granja
fast rápido/rápida
father el padre
feather la pluma
February febrero
fence la valla
ferry el ferry
field el prado
fifteen quince
finger el dedo
fire el fuego
fire engine el coche
  de bomberos
firefighter la bombera (f)
firefighter el bombero (m)
first primero/primera
fish (to eat) el pescado
fish (in water) el pez
fishing pescar
fishing boat el barco de pesca
five cinco
flag la bandera
flight attendant el/la auxiliar
  de vuelo (m/f)
floor el suelo

flower la flor
fly la mosca
foal el potro
fog la niebla
food la comida
foot el pie
football el balón de fútbol
football boots las botas
  de fútbol
football match el partido
  de fútbol
footballer el/la futbolista (m/f)
footstool el reposapiés
forest el bosque
fork el tenedor
four cuatro
fourteen catorce
fox el zorro
frame el marco
Friday viernes
fridge el frigorífico
friend la amiga (f)
friend el amigo (m)
friends las amigas (f)
friends los amigos (m)
frog la rana
fruit la fruta
fruit juice el zumo de fruta
full lleno/llena
furniture los muebles
galaxy la galaxia
game el juego
garage el garaje
garden el huerto
gardener el jardinero
gate la puerta de la verja
genie el genio
getting up levantarse
giant el gigante
giraffe la jirafa
girl la niña
glass el vaso
glasses las gafas
globe el globo terráqueo
gloves los guantes
glue el pegamento
goalkeeper el portero
goat la cabra
goggles las gafas
  de natación
going to sleep acostarse
gold dorado
good bueno/buena
goose el ganso
gorilla el gorila

grandfather el abuelo
grandma la yaya
grandmother la abuela
grandpa el yayo
grandparents los abuelos
grapes las uvas
grass la hierba
great-aunt la tía abuela
great-grandparents
  los bisabuelos
great-uncle el tío abuelo
green verde
greenhouse el invernadero
grey gris
grizzly bear el oso pardo
guitar la guitarra
gymnastics la gimnasia
hail el granizo
hair el pelo
hairbrush el cepillo del pelo
hairdresser la peluquera (f)
hairdresser el peluquero (m)
ham el jamón
hammer el martillo
hamster el hámster
hand la mano
handbag el bolso de señora
happy feliz
hat el sombrero
having a wash lavarse
hay el heno
he él
head la cabeza
head teacher el director (m)
head teacher la directora (f)
headache dolor de cabeza
headphones los auriculares
healthy sano/sana
heart el corazón
heavy pesado/pesada
hedge el seto
height la altura
helicopter el helicóptero
her ella
hexagon el hexágono
high jump el salto de altura
highchair la trona
hill la colina
him le
hippopotamus el hipopótamo
holiday el día festivo
home la casa
horse el caballo
hose la manguera
hospital el hospital

# English/inglés – Spanish/español

hot caliente
hotel el hotel
house la casa
hug abrazo
hugging abrazar
hundred cien
ice el hielo
ice-cream el helado
ill enfermo/enferma
in front of delante de
injection la inyección
instruments los instrumentos
jacket la chaqueta
jam la mermelada
January enero
jellyfish la medusa
jewellery box el joyero
jigsaw el rompecabezas
jobs los oficios
jogger el corredor (m)
jogger la corredora (f)
jug of water la jarra de agua
July julio
jumper el suéter
jumping saltar
June junio
jungle la jungla
kangaroo el canguro
key la llave
kid (baby goat) el cabrito
king el rey
kiss beso
kissing besar
kitchen la cocina
kite la cometa
kitten el gatito
kiwi el kiwi
knee la rodilla
knife el cuchillo
knight el caballero
koala el koala
ladder la escalera
lake el lago
lamb el cordero
lamp la lámpara
lampshade la pantalla
laptop el portátil
last último/última
lawn el césped
lawnmower el cortacésped
lawyer la abogada (f)
lawyer el abogado (m)
leaf la hoja
left izquierdo/izquierda
leg la pierna

lemonade la limonada
lemon el limón
letter la carta
lettuce la lechuga
level crossing el paso a nivel
library la biblioteca
life jacket el chaleco
  salvavidas
lifeguard el/la salvavidas (m/f)
lift el ascensor
light ligero/ligera
lighthouse el faro
lightning el relámpago
lion el león
lip el labio
lizard el lagarto
lobster la langosta
log el tronco
lollipop la piruleta
long largo/larga
long jump el salto de longitud
lorry el camión
lorry driver la camionera (f)
lorry driver el camionero (m)
luggage el equipaje
lungs los pulmones
magic lamp la lámpara mágica
magic set el juego de magia
magic wand la varita mágica
magician el mago
make-up el maquillaje
mango el mango
map el mapa
March marzo
market el mercado
mat la alfombrilla
May mayo
me mí
meal la comida
medicine la medicina
meerkat el suricato
mermaid la sirena
messy desordenado/
  desordenada
milk la leche
mini-golf el minigolf
mirror el espejo
mobile phone el móvil
model aeroplane
  la maqueta de avión
Monday lunes
money el dinero
monkey el mono
months los meses
moon la luna

morning la mañana
mosquito el mosquito
mother la madre
motorbike la motocicleta
mountain la montaña
mountain bike
  la mountain bike
mouse el ratón
mouse hole la madriguera del
  ratón
mouth la boca
Mr. Sr.
Mrs. Sra.
mud el fango
multicoloured multicolor
mum mamá
museum el museo
music la música
nail el clavo
nail varnish el esmalte
  de uñas
nails las uñas
name el nombre
napkin la servilleta
neck el cuello
necklace el collar
nephew el sobrino
niece la sobrina
night el noche
nightdress el vestido de noche
nine nueve
nineteen diecinueve
noisy ruidoso/ruidosa
nose la nariz
November noviembre
numbers los números
nurse la enfermera (f)
nurse el enfermero (m)
oar el remo
ocean el océano
October octubre
octopus el pulpo
office la oficina
old viejo/vieja
on en/sobre
one uno/una
onion la cebolla
operating theatre
  el quirófano
operation la operación
opposites los opuestos
orange (colour) naranja
orange (fruit) la naranja
orange juice el zumo de
  naranja

orbit la órbita
orchard el huerto
otter la nutria
oval ovalado/ovalada
owl el buho
paddle el remo
paddling pool la piscina
  de niños
paintbrush el pincel
painting pintar
painting el cuadro
paints las pinturas
pale pálido/pálida
palette la paleta
panda el panda
pants los calzoncillos
paper el papel
parents los padres
park el parque
park-keeper la jardinera (f)
park-keeper el jardinero (m)
parrot el loro
party la fiesta
party blower el matasuegras
party dress el vestido de fiesta
party hat el sombrero de fiesta
pasta la pasta
path el camino
pavement la acera
pavilion el pabellón
peach el melocotón
pear la pera
pedestrian crossing el paso
  de peatones
pen la pluma
pencil el lápiz
penguin el pingüino
petrol station la gasolinera
petshop la tienda
  de mascotas
picnic el picnic
picture el cuadro
pig el cerdo
pigeon el palomo
piglet el cerdito
pillow la almohada
pilot el piloto
pineapple la piña
pink rosa
pirate el pirata
pizza la pizza
planets los planetas
plant la planta
plant pot la maceta
plaster la tirita

**plate** el plato
**platform** el andén
**playground** el parque infantil
**playing** jugar
**plumber** el lampista
**pocket** el bolsillo
**pointing** señalar
**polar bear** el oso polar
**police car** el coche de policía
**police officer** el/la policía (m/f)
**poncho** el poncho
**pond** el estanque
**pony** el pony
**popstar** la estrella del Pop
**port** el puerto
**post office** la oficina
  de correos
**postbag** la bolsa del cartero
**postbox** el buzón
**poster** el póster
**postman** el cartero
**potato** la patata
**present** el regalo
**prince** el príncipe
**princess** la princesa
**pulling** tirar
**pupil** la alumna (f)
**pupil** el alumno (m)
**puppets** los títeres
**puppy** el cachorro
**purple** morado/morada
**purse** el monedero
**pushchair** el carrito
**pushing** empujar
**pyjamas** el pijama
**pyramid** la pirámide
**quadbike** el quad
**queen** la reina
**quiet** silencioso/silenciosa
**rabbit** el conejo
**race** la carrera
**racket** la raqueta
**racoon** el mapache
**radio** la radio
**rail station** la estación de tren
**rails** los raíles
**rain** la lluvia
**rainbow** el arco iris
**rake** el rastrillo
**rat** la rata
**reading** leer
**reading corner** el rincón
  de lectura
**recorder** la flauta
**rectangle** el rectángulo

**red** rojo/roja
**referee** el/la árbitro (m/f)
**refuse collector**
  la basurera (f)
**refuse collector**
  el basurero (m)
**reindeer** el reno
**remote control** el mando a
  distancia
**restaurant** el restaurante
**rhinoceros** el rinoceronte
**rice** el arroz
**right** derecho/derecha
**ring** el anillo
**river** el río
**road** la carretera
**road sign** la señal de tráfico
**robot** el robot
**rock** la roca
**rocket** el cohete
**rocking horse** el caballito
  balancín
**rollerblades** los patines
**rope** la cuerda
**roundabout** la rotonda
**rowing boat** el bote a remos
**rubber ring** el salvavidas
**rubber** la goma de borrar
**rucksack** la mochila
**rug** la alfombra
**ruler** la regla
**running** correr
**sack** el saco
**sad** triste
**salad** la ensalada
**sales assistant**
  el vendedor (m)
**sales assistant**
  la vendedora (f)
**same** igual
**sand** la arena
**sandals** las sandalias
**sandcastle** el castillo
  de arena
**sandpit** el cajón de arena
**sandwich** el bocadillo
**satchel** la cartera
**satellite** el satélite
**Saturday** sábado
**saucepan** la cacerola
**saucer** el platillo
**sauna** la sauna
**sausages** las salchichas
**saw** el serrucho
**scaffolding** el andamio

**scarecrow** el espantapájaros
**scarf** la bufanda
**school** la escuela
**scientist** la científica (f)
**scientist** el científico (m)
**scissors** las tijeras
**scoreboard** el marcador
**sculpture** la escultura
**seagull** la gaviota
**seasons** las estaciones
**seat** el asiento
**seaweed** el alga marina
**secretary** la secretaria
**see-saw** el balancín
**September** septiembre
**seven** siete
**seventeen** diecisiete
**shampoo** el champú
**shapes** las formas
**shark** el tiburón
**she** ella
**shed** el cobertizo
**sheep** la oveja
**sheepdog** el perro pastor
**sheet** la sábana
**shelf** la estantería
**shell** la concha
**shelter** el refugio
**shepherd** el pastor
**ship** el barco
**shirt** la camisa
**shoes** los zapatos
**shop** la tienda
**shopping bag** la bolsa de
  la compra
**short** corto/corta
**shorts** los pantalones cortos
**shoulders** los hombros
**shower** la ducha
**shuttlecock** el volante
**signal** la señal
**signpost** el cartel
**silver** plata
**singing** cantar
**sink** el fregadero
**sister** la hermana
**sitting** estar sentado
**sitting room** el salón
**six** seis
**sixteen** dieciséis
**skeleton** el esqueleto
**skiing** esquiar
**skipping rope** la cuerda
  de saltar
**skirt** la falda

**skis** los esquís
**skull** el cráneo
**sky** el cielo
**slide** el tobogán
**sling** el cabestrillo
**slippers** las zapatillas
**slow** lento/lenta
**small** pequeño/pequeña
**snack** la merienda
**snack bar** el bar
**snail** el caracol
**snake** la serpiente
**snow** la nieve
**snowman** el muñeco
  de nieve
**soap** el jabón
**socks** los calcetines
**sofa** el sofá
**son** el hijo
**space** el espacio
**space shuttle**
  el transbordador espacial
**spade** la pala
**speakers** los altavoces
**sphere** la esfera
**spider** la araña
**sponge** la esponja
**spoon** la cuchara
**sport** los deportes
**sports bag** la bolsa
  de deporte
**sports centre** el centro
  deportivo
**sports kit** el equipo de
  deporte
**spring** la primavera
**square** el cuadrado
**squirrel** la ardilla
**stains** las manchas
**stall** el tenderete
**standing** estar de pie
**star** la estrella
**starfish** la estrella de mar
**starting block** el taco
  de salida
**stethoscope**
  el fonendoscopio
**stick** el palo
**stilts** los zancos
**stitches** los puntos
**stones** las piedras
**stool** el taburete
**storm** la tormenta
**storybook** el libro de
  cuentos

## English/inglés – Spanish/español

strawberry la fresa
stream el arroyo
streamer la serpentina
suitcase la maleta
summer el verano
sun el sol
suncream la loción solar
Sunday domingo
sunglasses las gafas de sol
superhero costume
  el disfraz de superhéroe
supermarket el supermercado
surfboard la tabla de surf
surfer el/la surfista (m/f)
surgeon el/la cirujano (m/f)
swan el cisne
swimming nadar
swimming costume el traje
  de baño
swimming-pool la piscina
swing el columpio
table la mesa
table football el futbolín
table tennis el ping pong
tablet la tablet
tablets las pastillas
tadpole el renacuajo
talking hablar
taxi-driver el/la taxista (m/f)
tea el té
tea towel el paño de cocina
teacher la profesora (f)
teacher el profesor (m)
team el equipo
teapot la tetera
teddy bear el osito
  de peluche
teeth los dientes
telephone el teléfono
television la televisión
ten diez
tennis el tenis
tennis court la cancha
  de tenis
tent la tienda de campaña
textbook el libro de texto
thermometer el termómetro
thirteen trece
thousand mil
three tres
Thursday jueves
tiara la tiara
ticket el billete
ticket collector
  el cobrador (m)

ticket collector
  la cobradora (f)
tidy ordenado/ordenada
tiger el tigre
tights las medias
till la caja registradora
tissues los pañuelos
toast la tostada
today hoy
toe el dedo del pie
toilet el retrete
toilet paper el papel higiénico
toilets el váter público
tomato el tomate
tongue la lengua
toolbox la caja de
  herramientas
toothache dolor de muelas
toothbrush el cepillo
  de dientes
toothpaste la pasta
  de dientes
tornado el tornado
towel la toalla
town la ciudad
toy train el trenecito
  de juguete
toys los juguetes
toyshop la tienda de
  juguetes
track el sendero
tractor el tractor
traffic lights el semáforo
trailer el remolque
train el tren
train driver
  el/la maquinista (m/f)
transparent transparente
transport el transporte
travel el viaje
tree el árbol
treehouse la casita del árbol
triangle el triángulo
tricycle el triciclo
triplets los trillizos
trolley el carrito
trough el bebedero
trousers el pantalón
trowel la paleta
trumpet la trompeta
trunk el baúl
T-shirt la camiseta
tube el tubo
Tuesday martes
tummy la barriga

tummy ache dolor de barriga
tunnel el túnel
turquoise turquesa
twelve doce
twenty veinte
twins las gemelas (f)
twins los gemelos (m)
two dos
UFO el OVNI
ugly feo/fea
umbrella el paraguas
uncle el tío
under bajo
under the sea
  el fondo del mar
vacuum cleaner el aspirador
van la furgoneta
vase el florero
vegetable garden el huerto
vegetables las verduras
vehicles los vehículos
vet la veterinaria (f)
vet el veterinario (m)
vineyard la viña
violet violeta
violin el violín
visitors los visitantes
vivid vívido/vívida
waistcoat el chaleco
waiting-room la sala de
  espera
walking andar
walking boots las botas
walking stick el bastón
wall el muro
walrus la morsa
wardrobe el armario
washbasin el lavabo
washing machine la lavadora
washing-up la vajilla sucia
watch el reloj
watching TV ver la tele
water el agua
water butt la cisterna pluvial
waterfall la cascada
watering-can la regadera
wave la ola
weather el tiempo
Wednesday miércoles
weight el peso
wellington boots las botas
  de agua
wet mojado/mojada
whale la ballena
wheat el trigo

wheelbarrow la carretilla
wheelchair la silla de ruedas
whistle el silbato
white blanco/blanca
whiteboard la pizarra
wind el viento
window la ventana
winter el invierno
witch la bruja
wok el wok
wolf el lobo
wood la madera
worm la lombriz
wreck el naufragio
writing escribir
x-ray la radiografía
x-ray machine la máquina
  de rayos X
xylophone el xilófono
yacht el velero
yard el patio
year el año
yellow amarillo/amarilla
yesterday ayer
yoga el yoga
yogurt el yogur
you tú
young joven
zebra la cebra
zoo el zoo
zookeeper el/la guarda
  del zoo (m/f)

Published by b small publishing ltd.
Text and illustrations © b small publishing ltd. 2014

3 4 5 6 7 8 9 10

All rights reserved.

No part of this publication may be reproduced, stored
in a retrieval system, or transmitted, in any form
or by any means (including electronic, mechanical,
photocopying, recording, or otherwise) without prior
written permission from the publisher.

British Library Cataloguing-in-Publication Data
A catalogue record for this book is available
from the British Library.

Illustrations: Stu McLellan
Design: Louise Millar
Editorial: Sam Hutchinson and Susan Martineau
Spanish adviser: Diego Blasco Vázquez
Pronunciation guides: Catherine Bruzzone
Production: Madeleine Ehm
Printed in China by WKT Co. Ltd.

ISBN 978-1-909767-60-7

Please visit our website if you
would like to contact us.
www.bsmall.co.uk